Contents

Introduction

This is the personal story of an American, born in China and in love with the Great Earth of his early years, who served in China, Burma, and India as a soldier in World War II. Before my military experience, I was intensely pro-Chiang Kai-shek and an admirer of the Kuomingtang. But when I left China, I was convinced that Chiang and his party would lose China to the Communists, which they did.

I volunteered for army service at the ripe age of thirty-nine because I was sure our cause in Asia was just and because my younger brother had been killed by the Japanese in Java. I never doubted the justice of the American cause, but I became alienated by our Chinese Kuomingtang allies. I was horrified by the brutality of Chinese military discipline and by the open and cynical corruption of Chiang's regime in what we called Free China.

I went to China as a civil affairs officer. Since there was no need for an officer trained to govern conquered territory, I drifted from one assignment to another until I suddenly found myself attached to the Office of Strategic Services. This was a very tough organization, the forerunner of today's Green Berets and of the CIA. I was assigned by the OSS to Chiang's Secret Military Police, headed by General Tai Li. Here I was openly a double agent, working both for my own army and for the Chinese. Soon I became secretly a triple agent when I agreed to represent the three great Chinese secret societies (Triad) in their effort to secure American support to oust the Generalissimo and to establish a new moderate democratic government. This effort failed, and the Communists eventually ousted the corrupt Chiang regime because it was repudiated by a large proportion of the Chinese people.

Those of us who are critical of Chiang Kai-shek should not forget the enormous material progress which took place in China between 1927 and 1937 under his leadership. The Japanese attacked China in 1937 to destroy a potential rival. During the 1930s, industrial capitalism grew so fast in China as to pose a real challenge to Japanese dominance in East Asia. By attacking Chiang's China, Japan succeeded in destroying one rival but helped to create a much more dangerous one—the China of Mao Tse-tung.

Since I am critical of the Nationalists, I should state my position on the Communists in China. I saw something of their propaganda and their activities through the years in China, and I was not converted. I traveled extensively in Communist Europe and saw nothing there which attracted me to communism. Still later, I traveled in Latin America, the Middle East, Africa, Europe, and Asia where I was unavoidably aware of the nature of Communist strategy and its occasional successes.

I am convinced that international communism has not abandoned its basic Marxist goal of a world revolution which will open the door to world communism. I have received enough lectures from Communists in various parts of the world to believe they are quite sincere in their dogmatic and intolerant rejection of religion, of art as we know it, of democracy as we practice it, and of free enterprise. I believe them when they say communism and capitalism cannot exist together in the same world. I understand too well that to them "coexistence" is merely a peaceful interval which precedes the final collapse of capitalism. I did not favor the Communists over Tai Li. I said then, and repeat now, a plague on both their houses. I do believe there was an interval in time, late in 1944, when the United States could have changed the course of history by encouraging the moderate center groups in China to form a liberal democratic national government.

Mine was one of many American voices which pleaded for a change in our policies toward Chiang Kai-shek and Tai Li. Such a change was the only possible way to prevent Mao Tse-tung from conquering China. I had an opportunity to speak for the leaders of the secret societies; in so doing, I happened to be speaking also for millions of Chinese who were reacting against both the Nationalists and the Communists.

We all were defeated, and for twenty-five years it has been dangerous for an American to advocate new policies designed to build the foundation for renewed cooperation between the Chinese and American peoples. To understand this defeat, we must put a seventy-year-old U.S. position on China into perspective.

American policies toward China during this century have been influenced by sentimentality rather than reason—dominated by certain Old China Hands, of which there are three main varieties. Most numerous are the missionaries and the children of missionaries who admire the Chiangs because they are members of the Methodist church. Another powerful group consists of businessmen and military and naval personnel who supported Chiang and his Nationalist party because he was a strong man who had almost succeeded in unifying the country; under his authority business flourished and considerable material progress was achieved. And since his removal to Formosa, he has controlled an army which might be "unleashed" someday against Peking.

The third group is much smaller. It consists of Sinologists and some missionaries and their children who have been increasingly alienated by the absolutism of Chiang's dictatorship. This group is considered dangerous by a majority of Old China Hands. It never has had much influence in our China policies.

Between 1928 and 1944, when I returned to China in an army uniform, American policy strongly supported Chiang Kai-shek and the Nationalist government. Until President Nixon arrived on the scene, neither political disaster nor common sense has been able to shake the control of the sentimental oldsters who remember a China which no longer exists.

In 1944 I was still psychologically a member of the China Lobby. This was (and still is) a group of Old China Hands of the first two varieties who had spent a large part of their lives on the Chinese mainland and had had a deep emotional commitment to the Chinese people, reinforced by certain commercial interests. Possibly never has American national interest been so dominated by emotionalism and by the selfish economic interests of a small minority of Americans. Between 1944 and 1971 we seemed incapable of developing, understanding, and supporting a rational policy toward China. We refused to listen to the informed minority in the third group. The question for the future is whether a new and viable national policy toward China can be developed in the face of existing opposition.

I am a fairly typical Old China Hand. A kaleidoscope of memories made me an emotional ally of the Chinese people. The making of an Old China Hand may involve years of exposure to great food of infinite variety. It may involve years of tutoring in one of the world's beautiful languages and years of exposure to painting, sculpture, porcelain, lacquer, bronzes, and the other objects of beauty which are peculiarly Chinese. More than anything else, it requires many years of deep friendship with people to whom friendship is sacred and permanent. This process instills a deep and permanent love of another land and another people which overlooks human weakness and appreciates greatness. It also may cause one to overlook the inadequacy of their leaders.

A decisive experience in making me an Old China Hand occurred during the first year of the Sino-Japanese War in 1937. I was living with my family at a mountain resort, Mokanshan, when the Japanese army and navy attacked Shanghai, a hundred miles to the east. For weeks the air trembled with sound of distant artillery. We saw planes flying between us and the city. We were evacuated from the mountain to a coastal port where we boarded a British passenger ship. An American destroyer convoyed us to the mouth of the Hwangpu River below Shanghai. We arrived in the middle of a tremendous naval and ground attack on the Chinese positions; there appeared to be about one hundred Japanese warships offshore bombarding the Chinese army. Our captain steamed up the river in a complete blackout, interrupted by the constant flashing of the artillery like summer lightning. The air trembled and the ship shook as we steamed through the battle.

After establishing my wife and daughter with a missionary family, I hired a taxi which took me to my university in Nanking. Twice I made round trips through the battle lines from Nanking to Shanghai. The second time, I put my wife and child on a U.S. naval transport for a long trip home. My final return of one hundred and fifty miles back to Nanking was a nightmare of air raids, suffering civilians, hunger, and thirst.

For more than two months, I lived with a dozen other Americans in the Buck home at the university. We counted more than one hundred air raids during this time, some of them lasting eight hours. Much of the city was demolished. I found it somewhat nerve-wracking to teach a class in Shakespeare while I was looking out the window at a column of the black mushrooms created by bombs advancing directly toward us across the city. I was enormously impressed by the morale and courage of my Chinese students.

Once I reprimanded some students for going to sleep in class. Later one of them came to me and asked if I knew why they had gone to sleep. He explained that they had spent all of the previous night ministering to the thousands of wounded troops at the Hsiakwan railroad station. I was so ashamed of myself that I volunteered to spend a night in Hsiakwan myself.

I drove in the blackout through a dying city. I heard the wild screaming of a woman whom I could not help. Near the station, I heard a sound like the wind in a pine forest. It was the moaning of some three thousand wounded soldiers, lying in the cold November night, on a concrete station platform. The only food available was thin rice gruel. I spent the night talking to the dying, giving them water and a little food. Once when I was dipping some gruel from the cauldron, I was attacked by one of the walking wounded. A dying man shot through the stomach ordered him to stop, saying, "Can't you see he is a friend?" There was a long line of frail pine boxes. Two exhausted medical corpsmen picked up the dead and stacked them in these coffins. The stench was beyond belief. When morning came, I left in a state of shock.

I had decided to stay with the university for a year in order to secure an advance of salary to pay for the transportation of my wife and child to America. The administration announced plans to move bodily to Chengtu some one thousand miles to the west, near Tibet. As far as I know, I am the only American who traveled among some fifty million Chinese who fled before the Japanese army. We left Nanking in a British steamer which carried the priceless treasures of the Peking Imperial Palace museum in seven thousand crates to Free China. We also had three thousand half-starved refugees aboard. Because they wanted the treasure, the Japanese did not bomb us. Instead a column of armored cavalry tried to intercept us at a bend in the river at Wuhu, west of Nanking. We barely outran them and arrived in Hankow on a cold December morning. There I delivered to Ambassador Nelson Johnson a sealed briefcase which I had carried at the request of the only American who remained in the embassy in Nanking. The ambassador invited me to have coffee with him, something I had not enjoyed for three months. In Nanking, we had lived on powdered milk and a few vegetables from the garden and homemade bread for the duration of the siege.

The ambassador said to me, "Oliver, do you know what is going on?"

I replied that I thought a war had started which eventually would engulf the world.

"You are right, we are at the beginning of a thirty year war."

I asked him if he really thought the war would last thirty years. He said he was using a figure of speech, but that the war would involve all of mankind and it might last twenty, thirty, or fifty years. I asked him how he thought it would end, and I cannot forget his answer: "When Americans once again go to the well with a bucket for their water."

Eventually the faculty and students of the university, plus ten thousand books which I had selected from the library as the nucleus of a new library on a new campus in West China, took off in several smaller steamers for the spectacular trip through the Yangtze gorges. There is probably nothing like this steamer trip elsewhere in the world. In some places the great river flows in quiet lakes under mile-high cliffs. In other places it rages in wild rapids up which the sturdy little steamers inch their way, sometimes with the help of a donkey engine pulling on cables attached to rocks above the rapids.

At night we would anchor in some quiet cove surrounded by magnificent mountains. We traveled in relative luxury on shipboard. When we reached Chungking, I was shocked again to see the massive suffering of hundreds of thousands of refugees. There simply wasn't enough money, nor enough workers, nor enough food to take care of them.

It is three hundred miles by road from Chungking to Chengtu. I covered this trip in one long day in a truck. I learned that when thousands upon thousands die of starvation and disease, the last to die are the teenagers. The ditches on either side of the road were sometimes paved with the naked bodies of dead and dying youngsters. Those who still had the strength begged for help which I could not give them.

I was welcomed in the university city of Chengtu by old American friends from Nanking. Seeing the mental condition I was in, my friends suggested that we go for an extended weekend to a Taoist monastery in the foothills of the Himalayas.

After a short drive and a long walk, we came to what I will always remember as the Mountain of the Hand of God. Five gentle peaks like a thumb and four fingers surrounded a forested valley in which lay a very old temple. Orchids hung on the branches of trees in the mild February of this high valley. Paths led from the monastery to the forested fingers which protected it. There we looked westward at the first great snow ranges which guard Tibet. Far beneath us were caravans of Tibetans leading their yaks on a precipitous path down to the market place in the plain. Their shouts and songs echoed in the gorge.

The Chinese have traditionally looked to the mountains for beauty and healing. We were told that this mountain, whose real name I have lost, had been a religious center since 2700 B.C. It maintained austere but adequate living facilities for pilgrims, who could stay as long as they liked. There was no charge for food and lodging. When we left, we insisted on leaving a small contribution to the work of the religious community.

A monk of distinguished appearance, a gentle and well-educated man, acted as our host. We had four meals a day, culminating in a dinner at about four o'clock and supper at eight o'clock. The monastery owned thousands of acres of farmland at the foot of the mountain. The monks made wine from fruits which they raised, and cured ham in accordance with their own secret recipe. For three days I relaxed in this tranquil place; yet I could not properly sleep because I could not close my eyes without seeing the children dying.

The night before we were to return to the campus, we were kept awake all night by the blowing of trumpets and the chanting of the priests in some high festival. The next morning I asked our host rather sharply if it was necessary to keep people awake all night. He said that this was a special occasion, their yearly festival mass for the souls of all the people who had died the previous year. This year they had concentrated their prayers on the souls of all the soldiers who had died. I said to him, "But you must mean that you are praying only for the souls of Chinese soldiers."

He answered, "Oh no, we are also praying for the souls of our enemies for they, too, are men."

My healing began. I became a confirmed Old China Hand. And as such, in 1938, I returned to the United States where, until 1943 when I joined the army, I was a fanatical supporter of American intervention in the Sino-Japanese war on the side of China, certain that Chiang Kai-shek and Nationalist China were the defenders of freedom in East Asia. I had no strong opinion concerning the Chinese Communists because I had little personal knowledge of them. Like most Americans then, and now, any connection between reality and my concept of the Generalissimo and his government was purely accidential. For a hundred years, we have been backing the conservative political establishment against the growing pressures of social and economic revolution. We tried to prop Chiang up against the hostility of most of his people and we failed. We always lose when we try to stop the winds of change.

Twenty-six years after World War II, it appears that America has a chance to develop a new China policy, but I doubt if enough Americans know enough about China to develop and support a viable policy for the United States toward China. Until the recent past, when the few people who had a solid background in Chinese affairs have tried to influence American policy, they often have been persecuted. For years it has been dangerous to suggest that the misgovernment of Chiang and the Kuomingtang lost the support of the Chinese people on the mainland, and that no amount of American assistance, short of an all-out war, could have prevented the Communist conquest of China. When John Davies was driven out of the State Department into exile in Peru, the last scholarly, objective, and well-informed occupant of the China Desk disappeared. Since that time, good, well-meaning, but frequently ill-informed men have dominated our policies toward China, as they have most of the time since 1900.

Our national competence to evaluate Chinese affairs and to develop an intelligent and humane policy depends largely on the number of truly qualified China experts available and on the willingness of the American people to listen to them. Before Pearl Harbor, the U.S. Army, Navy, Marine Corps, and Foreign Service carefully trained selected men in Chinese-American affairs. These men spent up to four years in China studying the language and the culture in the context of their own professional background. Some of them became highly competent in Chinese language, philosophy, and literature.

Four years is not really long enough for an American to immerse himself in Chinese language and culture. China is too vast, its problems too complicated, and its language too difficult to be mastered in four years. But today we do not even have this source of supply of sane and relatively well-informed public servants. John Fairbank is quoted as saying that in a ten-year period recently, only five Americans secured a Ph.D. degree in Chinese affairs. Even a Ph.D. is not proof of adequate, intelligent competence when one is concerned with a quarter of the human race, five million square miles of territory, and five thousand years of history.

The fate of mankind may well be determined by what happens between China and the United States. Our national ignorance of China and the Chinese people is tragic. This ignorance is a formidable obstacle to rational communication between the United States and Communist China.

We always have been ignorant concerning China. This ignorance in 1944 and 1945 caused us stubbornly to support Chiang Kai-shek when he did not have the support of his own people. Our insistence on supporting Chiang made it impossible for Chinese moderates to replace Chiang's autocratic regime with a new moderate government. As a result, a large proportion of the Chinese people accepted the leadership of Mao Tse-tung.

My story—purposely episodic and told against the magnificent background of West China—describes this fateful, and fatal, period from 1944 to 1945. I tell it because I believe it is necessary for the American people to know at last of this virtually unknown, but historically important, incident of World War II so they may understand how wrong our national policies have been and still are in East Asia.

I ask that we try to understand and sympathize with the common man in China and in East Asia. I ask America to abandon permanently all efforts at military intervention on the Asian mainland. There are too many Asians and too few Americans.

Oliver J. Caldwell

Carbondale, Illinois
October 1971

A SECRET WAR

I ask the indulgence of professional Sinologists for any errors of omission or commission in this book. This applies particularly to the transliteration of Chinese names of people and places. I have tried to adhere to standard practice in spelling these names according to the Romanization of Wade, however, the names of most of the places and many of the people were noted orally on the spot, and sometimes the written Chinese characters were not available. Pronunciations were frequently quite different from the generally accepted norm—Mandarin as it is spoken in Peking.

Prologue

On a cold December day in 1943, I sailed from Newport News on a liberty ship into a howling blizzard. The storm lasted a week and protected us from German submarines. I was a one-man shipment. My number was RF-705. Most shipment numbers designated companies, or battalions, or larger groups. The troop transport officers I met were mystified by my solitary designation. No one would tell me where I was going. All I knew was that I was headed in the direction of India and China.

After sundry mishaps, shipment RF-705 found himself in Algiers on board a decrepit Dutch passenger liner which had been condemned to the scrap heap just before the beginning of the European War. Between submarine scares and air raid alarms, I organized an orientation class for officers on their way to China. I thought this was a laudable idea; it seemed obvious that these young men should not be deposited on the Chinese side of the Hump without some concept of what it was going to be like and how they should act to get along with the Chinese people. After a few days my orientation class fell apart because one young officer denounced me to Army intelligence as a Chiang Kai-shek agent. His reasoning was simple. I spoke well of Chiang's China. Therefore I must be a traitor to my own country.

I expected to find out in New Delhi where I was going and what I would do. To my embarrassment, no one in General Stilwell's headquarters would admit that they had ever heard of me. Eventually I learned that I had been scheduled originally to assist in setting up military government in Burma following its conquest by British and American forces. Somebody, probably Stilwell himself, had vetoed the idea because it would not be politically advisable for an American officer to be part of a British colonial government. Therefore, RF-705 received orders to go to China.

Getting from India into China during most of World War II was an adventure. Local air force officers told me that in 1944 about a thousand American planes, and the troops and supplies in them, went down in the wild mountains separating India from China.

I arrived at the Chabua Airfield in an elated mood. The plane which had transported a handful of officers and men from Calcutta had flown for several hundred miles in crystal clear weather, parallel to the high peaks of the Himalayas. The pilot first delivered a heavy stone crusher to Johor; it was apparently a gift from the U.S. Army to the sultan. After we refueled the pilot asked my permission as senior officer aboard to fly north to the mountains and to follow them up to northern Assam. We came in over Nepal, near the great pyramid of Makalu, then flew northeast past Everest and Kanchenjunga for several hundred miles parallel to mountains whose names are seldom printed in the Western world. As we approached the last immense mountain, Namcha Barwa, a long twenty-five-thousand-foot ridge of purest white, the pilot went into a glide down to the steaming plain in which our airfields were located. These air bases supported our army in China.

The monsoon hit us that afternoon and obliterated everything but the soggy wet jungle which surrounded the base. The next day about twenty of us were called together and given our orders. We were about to fly the Hump. An officer issued survival kits consisting of a pistol and ammunition, emergency rations, and drugs and bandages.

He told us to cheer up, that there was only one chance in ten that our plane would go down in the wilderness which separated us from China. Furthermore, he maintained that even if we went down, we had a better than even chance to walk out alive.

He also told us our plane had to be overloaded by 60 percent in order to reach Kunming with a useful payload. Therefore, we could not fly above eighteen thousand feet, but the mountain peaks ahead of us rose to about twenty-three thousand feet. If they were covered with storms, which generally was the case, then the pilot had to fly by dead reckoning. If he guessed wrong, you collided with an arctic mountaintop.

Another hazard was the existence of a few Japanese planes which liked to hunt down our unarmed transports when the weather was good. One-eyed Charlie was the name of a particularly dangerous Japanese pilot; he liked to fly close to an American plane to inspect it before shooting it down. This enabled some of the occupants to bail out; some of them managed to return to Assam to tell stories about One-eyed Charlie.

We took off one morning in a badly overloaded C-46, a plane which I always regarded with profound suspicion after my initial adventure on this flight. We reached fourteen thousand feet, where it was bitter cold, flying without a door in order to facilitate parachuting in case we encountered One-eyed Charlie.

I saw in front of us a huge snow mountain. The plane was headed for a pass which led into the gorge of the Irrawaddy River. Just before we reached the pass one engine conked out. The pilot should have turned around and gone back to Chabua. Instead, he decided he would proceed over the pass and try to start the engine on the other side. We lost altitude rapidly but managed to skim over the tops of Christmas trees sticking up through the snow. On the other side of the pass, we hit a down draft and dropped four thousand feet into the gorge. Immediately ahead of us was a wall of rock ranging thousands of feet into the clouds.

I sat by the crew chief, a sergeant, who took a post-card out of a pocket and wrote a farewell note addressed to "My darling wife." He showed it to me as he returned it to a pocket of his flight jacket on the off chance that some one would find it on his body. We then lined up to jump and I was given the privilege of making the first exit.

As I prepared to throw myself out into space for my first parachute jump, strangely enough with no fear at all, the sergeant told me to hold up, that the pilot would try to make a turn on one engine. This was theoretically impossible, loaded as we were. He gunned his port engine until the old plane trembled and managed a 180° turn, after which we flew at about eight thousand feet down the Irrawaddy gorge toward Japanese-held Burma.

The pilot sent word back that he would try to ditch the plane in the first straight stretch of level water he could find. We then would swim ashore and walk for a few weeks until we found a friend. But he could not find any straight stretch of calm water in that river so we went on and on. Suddenly the mountains ended and we found ourselves flying over Myitkyina, a small town in northern Burma. There was a Japanese airfield on each side of the town. We flew low enough over one field to see soldiers running to their antiaircraft guns and pilots of fighter planes preparing to take off. The Japanese apparently decided we were a dying duck not worthy of wasted ammunition. For three more hours, we flew low on one engine over the hills and jungles of the Shan country of northern Burma.

By this time, morale was bad. Suddenly the dead engine came to life and we soared like a sea gull into the sky. The pilot told us to look at a tremendous bank of clouds directly ahead of us. "Everyone pray that it isn't full of rocks," he commanded.

We prayed and it wasn't. On the other side, we came out into the clear, blue sky of Southwest China. On almost our last drop of gasoline, we landed at Kunming. We left the plane for a truck which drove us to our quarters. This was the first time I saw men wearing light green complexions. The pilot and copilot were both in a state of shock.

The next morning I went to the colonel in charge of personnel. He had no idea why I had been sent to China. I told him I could speak Mandarin and Foochow and had a smattering of other dialects. Also, I knew a lot of people in the government of China and in its universities, and I had published a number of papers on education and political affairs in China. In addition, I said I had scored 100 percent in an army examination in spoken Japanese at the University of Chicago Civil Affairs School. The colonel told me to come back the next day.

So I did, and he said he had talked to the general about me and the general (affectionately known as "Pinky" Dorn) said he didn't need another officer on his staff who knew about China. I was to wait until the general could find something worthy of my talents. I got the impression that Old China Hands were not welcome in the U.S. Army in China. This fact was made very clear to me many times in the next two years.

From Kunming I was ordered to go to Chungking where I was to live at the USIS house. Here, I was assigned to work with Colonel Archibald Fisken in teaching English to Chinese who would serve as interpreters for the American army in China. My experience in this assignment cooled my previous enthusiasm for Chiang Kai-shek's government.

The colonel and I were under the general direction of the minister of information of the Chiang Kai-shek government. He was Hollington Tong; I had known him before the war in Nanking. Hollington assigned the colonel and me to teach English to several hundred college students who had been drafted and who were being trained in what had been a concentration camp where President Chiang's government had previously sent his political opponents. In the National Central Political Training Institute, they benefited from a routine designed to improve their characters and their method of thinking. Incidentally, we were supposed to teach them some English.

I looked forward to an opportunity to make an honest contribution to the winning of our war.

1 Mr. Chen

It was springtime in China in 1944. We were sitting in the living room of the Office of War Information headquarters in Chungking, listening to a recording of *Oklahoma*. I was thinking that America had finally developed an indigenous art form, a new folk opera, when the Number One Boy came in and whispered that a Mr. Chen was waiting outside to see me.

Mr. Chen was an elderly gentleman, attired in a light blue scholar's gown. He was lean and wiry and had the assurance and dignity which characterize older Chinese scholars. He was on the staff of the National Central Political Training Institute where I was teaching English to former Chinese college students who were being trained to serve as interpreters for American forces in China. He invited me to take a walk with him on the following Sunday morning to a monastery ten miles outside Chungking. He would treat me to Sunday dinner at the temple, which was famous for its Buddhist cuisine.

I told him I was honored by his invitation but curious as to the reason he wanted to take an American officer whom he knew slightly on such an excursion. He said he had an important matter to discuss with me. I asked him what he wanted to talk about; he replied that this was not an appropriate time and place for the discussion he had in mind. I had been selected to receive certain information because I had lived so long in China and spoke Mandarin. He thought I would be better able to understand the problem he wished to discuss than an American officer with a different background. I accepted the invitation and went back to the group listening to *Oklahoma*, which included some of the best men USIS employed in China, most of whom resigned shortly after the end of hostilities.

When the concert was over, I told one of them, a man who later gained prestige as a literary critic in New York, that I had had a strange invitation to go on a long walk next Sunday. Two young Americans who also were teaching English at the institute, and who had been through crash Chinese language programs at American universities, asked if they could go with me. I told them I was Mr. Chen's guest for dinner but I had no reason to feel he would object to their joining us on the walk to the monastery.

I was wrong. This Sunday morning in late spring in Chungking was fair and cool. Mr. Chen arrived about nine o'clock and was displeased that the other two Americans were joining us. He said we would have to walk fast and get out of their hearing, since what he had to say to me was for my ears alone. He told me he was a Presbyterian minister, that he was sixty years old, and that he had a matter of great importance to tell me in the hope that I would pass the word on to our president in Washington. I told him that he was very flattering but I was only a captain in the army of the United States, a man of no influence, and he should tell his story to somebody who could help him.

He answered that he and his friends had many times tried unsuccessfully to discuss their problem with representatives of the American embassy and with people in General Stilwell's headquarters. For security reasons, they had not talked to other junior officers, and they were unable to reach anyone with authority. Mr. Chen then told me that he knew exactly what I was doing in Chungking (which was more than I knew), and that I had access to people who could evaluate his story and act appropriately.

ber was destitute, his guild cared for him and his family. If he died his society buried him. Such guilds were found in many large cities in China and exercised considerable political and social influence.

I am writing in the past tense because Mao Tse-tung has relentlessly persecuted the secret societies. Under a Communistic government only the Communist party officially may be secret. It is my opinion, however, that the major secret societies probably went underground, as they reportedly did sometimes in the past when an old dynasty died and a new one came into power.

Trade guilds also were powerful in Old China. The goldsmiths were members of an organization which controlled prices, set standards, and, in general, governed the trade. A man could not carry on business in this field unless he was a member of the guild. If he tried, he could be murdered. This system was similar to the guilds of the Middle Ages in Europe. Much of the wealth of China was concentrated in the hands of guild chiefs. They sometimes made or broke governments.

When Chiang Kai-shek captured Shanghai in 1927 while he was on his march north to unify China, he made a deal with the guild chiefs of Shanghai, whereby they backed his government and made a large cash advance to him. In return, he crushed the labor unions which had threatened to upset the traditional guild economy of the city.

Some of the most powerful secret societies seemed to be protective brotherhoods which men joined to get a little security for their families. For example, the Red Spears were a group about which relatively little is known, but which appeared to consist of farmers banded together to protect themselves against bandits and oppressive government. They had secret ceremonies and a mystic doctrine which involved incantations to protect them from the bullets of their better armed adversaries. They went forth at night to attack their enemies. They fought the Japanese when the Japanese were foolish enough to bother them. They also fought the Nationalists and the Communists impartially when occasion required. The Red Spears existed chiefly in the middle and lower valley of the Yellow River.

There were also societies in China with a religious background. One of the oldest of these was the Society of the White Lotus, the Pai Lien Hui. This was a secretive organization about which little was ever known in the West except that it consisted apparently of ardent Buddhists.

In the seventeenth century, after the fall of the Ming dynasty, the members of the White Lotus became a revolutionary group opposed to the new, foreign, Manchu emperor. They fought an underground war for decades and were finally driven so far under that some modern authorities doubt if the order survived.

An American missionary of my acquaintance may be the only white man who has attended a meeting of the Society of the White Lotus. He described the chapter he knew as a group of mystics who helped each other along the way of Buddhist salvation. They dressed in ceremonial garments and recited the Sutras together. He saw them sacrifice a white cock in dedicating a statue of the Buddha. The body of the rooster was buried inside the statue as a symbol of eternal life. He told me part of the ritual closely paralleled certain Masonic rituals.

I know of no evidence that the White Lotus took part in the struggle for power in modern China, but another

Buddhist society has done so. The Red Swastika Society was a Buddhist equivalent of the Red Cross societies of Europe and America. It was nominally more interested in the next world than in this one, but there was reason to believe that on occasion it took part in world events in China.

The Catholics had to organize for survival in Northwest China in a manner perhaps unknown elsewhere. They built fortified Christian villages, and organized a secret service which was an excellent source of military information during the war. This secret service was apparently designed to spy on the Communists who were regarded as the chief enemies of the Church. It would be interesting to know if this group still operates in the Church which now exists in Mao's China.

The largest Chinese secret organizations are hard to describe in American terms. The head of the Green Circle, the Ch'ing Pan in 1944, was a gentleman named Tu Yusung. He was reputed to be a native of Shanghai; men in his position were not willing for all the facts about their lives to be made known. At one time he was the Al Capone of Shanghai and controlled the dope and prostitution rackets. He had a fine home in the French Concession where he could not be touched by the Chinese police since he was in French territory.

Tu branched out into a new field when labor in Shanghai began to unite. Wages and working conditions in Shanghai were among the worst in the world. The millowners were getting rich off slave labor and did not want any changes made. They made an agreement with Tu whereby he headed off any inconvenient activities by the workers. He became the labor boss of Shanghai.

One of the most profitable activities for a racketeer,

in China as well as America, was kidnapping. Tu Yu-sung's boys were experts. Even under the protection of foreign police in the Concessions, a rich man was not safe. There were too many ways of avenging oneself on a man's family. Tu's victims generally paid up and kept quiet. So Tu became one of the greatest men in Old International Shanghai. The *Who's Who for China* printed his picture captioned "Banker and Philanthropist."

One day the Generalissimo and his Madame came to visit Shanghai. It seemed that the visitors, the first family of China, did not show enough deference to Tu Yu-sung. He sent a note to Chiang suggesting that possibly the Madame needed "protection" while she was in Shanghai, hinting that Tu would be happy to provide it for a nominal fee. The Generalissimo said, "No." Shortly thereafter, a note was delivered to Madame Chiang asking her to go immediately to the home of her sister; Madame Kung was sick, and had sent a limousine to pick up her younger sister and carry her through the dangers of Shanghai to the Kung home. So Madame Chiang put on her coat and got in the car. She wasn't seen again by her family for some time.

When the Generalissimo came home, there was no wife to greet him. He heard the story, and put two and two together. He phoned Tu's office and that gentleman told him that quite by accident some of Tu's men had seen Madame Chiang riding around the streets of Shanghai in a strange motorcar, so they had taken her into protective custody. Of course the boys had spent much valuable time in protecting the good lady, and no doubt General Chiang would be glad to reimburse them for their services. This he did, turning over a large ransom worthy of the parties involved. The Madame came home no worse for the adventure. Thereafter, the Chiangs paid tribute for the privilege of visiting Shanghai. Tu's position was secure.

The Green Circle spread through the Yangtze Valley at least as far as Chungking. It became one of the powerful forces in modern China prior to the Sino-Japanese war, yet its very existence was unknown to most of the foreigners who lived in the port cities it infested. It was interested in any easy way to make money, such as selling opium and heroin and little peasant girls, murder, and breaking labor unions. But it continued to be an umbrella under which the farmers and merchants of rural China could find some protection in an age of disorder. It also maintained strong ties with several Buddhist orders.

As the organization grew stronger, it seemed to grow more respectable. Possibly Tu Yu-sung wanted to be able to face his ancestors with a better conscience. It accepted into its brotherhood a certain number of decent men. Such men generally joined as a matter of protection for themselves and their families.

When I knew it, the Green Circle was said to consist of about four thousand "sworn brothers," and about four million lesser members. The "brothers" were the officers, the many were the enlisted men. This is how one respectable man became one of the "brothers."

His family was rich, and his father was afraid that the Green Circle might kidnap one of his children. One of the sons was appointed to become a "sworn brother" of the society, which never would attack a member in good standing. This man later went to a university, and to America for graduate study. He became a prominent and respected member of the progressive intellectuals in East China. All the time he was one of the four thousand "brothers." It paid off, as the family was never molested. The society must have received something in return for this immunity.

When Japan attacked China in 1937, the Green Circle had become one of the most powerful forces in Central China. It was natural for both the Chinese government and the Japanese to bid for the support of such an organization. There is reason to believe that the Green Circle was predominantly loyal and anti-Japanese. After all, it had officially supported Chiang for ten years. However, the Green Circle did enough for the Japanese to win the trust of the invaders and to be able to continue its operations in Shanghai area with little hindrance. But Tu Yu-sung, gentleman banker and philanthropist, moved to Lanchow in the far Northwest. There he was safe from both the Japanese and the Generalissimo.

In South China, the Red Circle, or Hong Pan was in many ways similar to the other Circle in the North. The southern society was probably smaller; it was supposed to have about two million members. Before the Japanese moved into China, the headquarters of the Red Circle was in Canton, with branch operations in Hongkong and in other southern cities. After the Japanese invasion, the headquarters moved to Kweilin, and here it controlled much of the great smuggling industry and almost everything else that went on underground.

After the fall of Kweilin, the leaders moved up into the Northwest. During the summer of 1945 the head man was reputed to be in Sian. His name was Ming Teh. I never saw his name in characters but assume that it means Bright Virtue. I believe I met him in Sian. At any rate, I did meet a tall, handsome man with a shaven head wearing a monk's costume who offered the cooperation of an unnamed secret group in guerrilla activities against the Japanese.

Some of China's secret societies were founded primarily for patriotic and benevolent purposes. One of these was the Ko Lao Hui, the Society of Elder Brothers, the third society in the Triad. I was told that Sun Yat-sen was a member of this society; through it he fought the Manchu dynasty during the years he was in exile. It contributed to the success of the Chinese revolution in 1911. When there was no longer a rebellion to foster, it became a philanthropic organization with political overtones; its membership seemed to consist primarily of comparatively wealthy merchants. Chiang Kai-shek became the nominal leader of the Ko Lao Hui. The actual leader, according to Mr. Chen, was the Christian General, Feng Yu-shan.

The Elder Brothers were strong in Szechwan and the Northwest. An American diplomat who wanted to study conditions in this area put himself in the hands of this society and was well satisfied with the results. He traveled safely and quickly wherever he wanted to go. There were some less pleasant stories of the activities of this organization. Sometimes it appeared to be a Fascist front. It sponsored a junior society for young people which sometimes acted like the Hitler Jugend. Since there were no Jews to attack, the target consisted of those who were considered lukewarm in their support of the Generalissimo.

All the organizations that have been mentioned were private and nongovernmental. There were several strong secret groups which were identified with the government of Chiang Kai-shek. One was the Whampoa Cadets, a secret organization of graduates of Chiang's old military academy in Canton. Then there were the Blue Shirts which were modeled after the various Shirt organizations of contemporary Europe. The Blue Shirts spied on everyone and treated with proper cruelty those they considered dangerous. They sat in university classrooms and reported teachers and students who were bold enough to express unorthodox ideas. The government had several secret services corresponding to the FBI. The two best known were the organization operated by the Ministry of Communications, under Hsu En-tsun, and the powerful Secret Military Police headed by General Tai Li.

In some ways, Tai Li was the most powerful man in China during World War II. He was said to be the only man who was permitted to go armed into the presence of the Generalissimo. He was the sword arm of the conservative clique in the Kuomingtang government. He was the archenemy of the Communists and of all liberals. Men like Tai Li do not tell the world much about themselves. He was particularly reticent. He was so quiet many American Old China Hands never heard of him. He was seldom seen in public. But when the going was bad for the Kuomingtang, he and his troops were likely to appear mysteriously and cause much harm to those who were known to hold dangerous democratic ideals.

According to tradition Tai Li was born in Chekiang province, not far from the ancestral home of Chiang Kai-shek. Little is known of his early life until he turned up as captain of Military Police in Shanghai in 1927, the year when Chiang led his revolutionary army north from Canton. When Chiang reached Shanghai, he denounced the Communists who had backed him to this point. It was true that the Communists committed excesses in Nanking and elsewhere. Chiang used these excesses as an excuse to eliminate them. He appears never to have trusted the Communists and he did not need their support any longer. Anyway, he had to eliminate them in order to secure a loan from the Shanghai bankers and guild chiefs to finance his new government.

There were a number of people to be killed and young Tai Li proved to be a highly efficient executioner. According to reports of this time, some of which were incorporated in Andre Malraux's novel, *Man's Fate,* he invented a new and efficient method of killing Chiang's enemies. He lined up some locomotives on a siding, got the fireboxes red hot, opened their doors, tied down the whistles to shut out the screams, and one after another threw his living victims into the fiery furnaces. According to tradition, thousands of labor leaders and students and intellectuals were killed in a few days. A good many of them may have been Communists. Thus Tai Li earned the nickname of the Butcher.

From this time forward, Tai Li made himself increasingly indispensable to Chiang Kai-shek. He always kept personally in the background, which seems to have been a good policy; no one could accuse him of too much ambition. He was one of the most feared and detested men in China. Abroad, he was almost unknown.

When the war started, Tai Li had a brilliant idea. He called together Tu Yu-sung, Ming Teh, Feng Yu-shan, and leaders of smaller societies, and proposed that they all form a united front of secret organizations to carry on a secret war against the Japanese. Intelligence nets would be formed behind the Japanese lines of communication. Everyone would work together for the welfare of China. This would actually be a formalizing of an informal arrangement which had existed since 1927. The leaders of the various secret organizations agreed to accept Tai Li's proposal. Because he represented the Generalissimo and the Chinese regular army, Tai Li was elected head of the coalition of secret societies.

For a while things apparently went smoothly. Nearly everyone was patriotic in the early days of the war. Intelligence nets were organized and guerrilla bands operated successfully at great cost to the Japanese. But as the years went on, something went wrong. Tai Li had a tremendous weapon in his hands. He used it to strengthen his control of the Chinese people rather than to fight the common enemy. It was easy to do this through the *pao-chia* system. Representatives of his united front of secret societies were able to crush liberal thought almost before it was born. It was the boast of the organization that there was not a single village in China in which there was not a Tai Li spy to report on subversive activities. By terrorizing a man's family it was easy to keep the man in line.

Several concentration camps were established to take care of thinkers of dangerous thoughts. There was one in Kweichow where intellectuals were confined until they saw the error of their ways. I heard of one professor, a man famous in economics, who was held there for several years because he expressed heretical beliefs concerning the Chinese tax system, which was hard on the poor and easy on the rich. There was another camp near Sian which catered particularly to students. When campus spies reported that certain students were getting out of hand, they were spirited away to this camp where they learned to be good democrats. There were other camps and prisons. Sometimes common jails were used. There was no right of habeas corpus.

The Secret Military Police of China was frankly modeled after the Gestapo. There was a time when China was under strong German influence. General Von Falkenhausen was head of a large mission which taught the Chinese army to goose-step and gave the Chinese much other useful information. The conservative clique, the group which dominated the Kuomingtang for many years, absorbed German ideals greedily.

Many otherwise well-informed Americans refused to believe the strength of the Nazi influence in China. There were thousands of men in the government of China during World War II who were trained in Germany, Russia, Italy, and, above all, Japan. Their ideals were often the ideals of the military cliques of those countries. This influence started from the top; the Generalissimo was educated in Japan, and his life and his thinking show the effect of his early training. The Tai Li Police was an organization intrinsically foreign to American institutions. It was influenced by the Gestapo, by the Japanese thought control organization, and by other similar outfits which were studied by Tai Li representatives.

As a result of years of skillful maneuvering, Tai Li brought the principal secret organizations of China under his control. In the name of patriotism they united under his leadership. This gave him a superb weapon to support his personal ideas and ambitions. Under his command were perhaps seven to eight million men in his own organization, and the affiliated secret societies. They blanketed

China. If Tai Li had used his weapon against Japan, he should have been able to drive them back into the coast cities, and to have freed completely the Chinese interior. Instead, it was used primarily against the Chinese people, to stamp out opposition against the Generalissimo, to spy on the Communists, to prepare for a future civil war when Japan had finally been defeated by the United States. As we shall see, it also was used to oppose American programs and policies in Asia. There were a few instances in which the Tai Li organization did actually fight the Japanese. Apparently this happened when it seemed altogether necessary, or when an individual commander really wanted to fight.

The Tai Li grip on the three major secret societies, each of which was much larger than his organization, was probably never very secure. As the years passed, and it became obvious that he was using the coalition to his own advantage, his influence lessened. But by then, he had the backing of the United States, and nothing could be done about it by the Chinese common people.

With the cooperation of the U.S. Navy, the Sino-American Cooperative Organization was created; Tai Li was the senior Chinese officer in SACO. His American counterpart was Commodore "Mary" Miles. Thus Tai Li reached the apex of his power. He was the Generalissimo's personal representative in dealing with American secret agencies. He was strongly supported by the U.S. Navy. His organization spied on and controlled American activities in China.

After the conquest of Shanghai, where he won important support from the bankers, the guilds, and the secret societies, Chiang quickly captured Peking and became president of Nationalist China. During the first ten years of Chiang's rule, great progress was made in China. Tens of thousands of miles of roads, suitable for cars, trucks, and buses, were built where only footpaths had existed. Education was expanded, agriculture and commerce both increased. These were relatively good years, marred by the growing Communist revolt and increasing pressure from Japan. The Japanese did not want China to become free and strong.

In rural China the societies maintained relative law and order so that Chiang could concentrate his attention on national and foreign affairs. But, Mr. Chen said, Chiang seemed to forget the debt he owed to the societies, and the common people they represented, when he became rich and powerful. Chiang forgot about the farmers; he seemed to forget that the farmers were 90 percent of China's population.

After Japan attacked China in 1937, for the first few years of the war the societies united with Tai Li to support Chiang's armies. Because of this support, Chiang was generally secure in his lines of communication and transportation. He possessed a network of loyal representatives in the territories conquered by the Japanese. After Chiang was compelled to leave Nanking and had established his wartime capital in Chungking, an estrangement grew between the secret societies and the Kuomingtang; Chiang used his secret police under Tai Li to crush opposition among his former supporters.

There were three issues, according to Mr. Chen. The first was Chiang's system of taxation which added 10 percent tax in kind on farm produce to the already slim profit margin of the average Chinese farmer. About half of all

Chinese farmers were tenants and turned over 40 or 50 percent of their produce to their landlords. The tax meant the difference between starvation and survival. By 1944, much of rural Free China was ready to revolt against Chiang Kai-shek. Another source of concern was Chiang's trading with the Japanese while pretending to fight them. Chiang's government was sending foodstuffs which the country could not spare through certain carefully preserved channels to the Japanese army, which repaid him with automobiles, machinery, and luxury goods. Finally, the village elders and the landlords, who were the backbone of the societies, were alarmed by the growing influence of the Chinese Communist party. The more the tenant farmers suffered, the more they were attracted by Communist propaganda.

Mr. Chen proposed to me that I, an obscure captain, advise my government that the breaking point had come, that the societies could no longer back Chiang Kai-shek. Mr. Chen wanted me to send word to President Roosevelt that if the United States continued to support Chiang Kai-shek, the only possible outcome would be a Communist China.

The societies proposed an alternative, the establishment of a moderate new government under the presidency of General Li Tsong-jen of the Southwest China command. General Li held the title of vice-president of China. The societies had formed an alliance with certain intellectuals in the universities, who were equally disturbed by Chiang's policies. Li had agreed to accept the presidency and to save Chiang's face by making him honorary president. Since Li was commander of the strongest army in China, with some three hundred to six hundred thousand soldiers, he could be counted on to command the allegiance of most of the Nationalist military forces. There would be a peaceful *coup d'etat*. Li would take over, a Communist revolution would be averted, trade with the Japanese would be cut off, and the enemy thereby weakened. Chinese and American forces would then join to drive the Japanese out of China.

I wondered how many middle-aged American army captains had received such a proposition. I told him I would think about it; he said he would keep in touch with me.

"In the meantime," he said, "I want to put you under the protection of the Society of Elder Brothers. I will give you our password and if you ever need help in your travels in this country, especially if you are trying to escape from the Japanese, you will go to the nearest village, walk down the main street, identify the biggest and most prosperous shop and ask to see the proprietor. When he appears, you will ask him this question: 'Wo-ti lao kung tsai nar' [where is my old uncle]."

I would then be taken under the protection of the society.

2 The National Central Political Training Institute

The Chinese National News Agency had issued feature stories relating how the senior students of several of China's leading universities had unanimously volunteered for service with the United States Army as interpreters. It was a nice story, but it was a lie. The senior men of National Central University, National Chungking University, and National Fuh Tan University had been conscripted, with little warning, and much against the will of most of them. They had valid reasons to object.

Students had for years been denied any general participation in the war; they were now suddenly thrown into it regardless of their wishes or qualifications. Many of the boys had practically no English. Less than 10 percent of them were actually qualified to become interpreters. Many of them were advanced students in law, engineering, and other specialized fields. They were plucked out of their academic careers three months before graduation. To get their degrees they would have to enroll again as students after the war.

They were given plenty of rank, but miserable salaries. It was a policy of the Chinese Nationalist Army to outrank Americans whenever possible. Most of these boys were captains and majors, although they had received little or no military training. Their average monthly pay was equivalent to fifteen dollars in American money. Their salaries were not raised as fast as inflation increased the cost of living. This system destroyed their self-respect. 'This same system helped later to destroy Chiang Kai-shek's army; it made graft a respectable necessity.

The boys objected to being shanghaied into the interpreters' program because they were afraid of the consequences. They knew they were expected to report on the activities and thoughts of the Americans they would work with. They expected to be assigned to various Chinese secret service agencies. It was sometimes difficult to get out of such agencies alive.

Prior to the general conscription, the head of the Interpreters Training Program, an affable and high ranking Chungking official, paid a visit to the boys in training at National Central University. There were two American officers there, who told me the dignitary had a very embarrassing time when he tried to give the boys a pep talk. Most of the seats were empty, an insult in itself, and the students who were there acted in a distressingly democratic manner.

Discipline is the dominant principle of the philosophy of the Generalissimo. Someone reported to him what had happened and he made a surprise visit to the campus. He was in a white-hot rage. He beheld various indications of poor discipline, and when he returned to his headquarters, he issued a decree that all the students being trained as interpreters would forthwith be removed to the National Central Political Training Institute, where they would receive concentrated military discipline and party political training, as well as a certain amount of English.

The National Central Political Training Institute was a large military camp occupying a valley and a mountainside above the Yangtze River about two miles outside Chungking. One entered through a monumental gate, then descended the mountain on well-kept footpaths. There were many long, low barracks and two-story classroom buildings. Down by the river was a large parade ground where the Generalissimo held reviews of his troops and of the trainees. An auditorium and offices were set in an attractive garden above the parade ground.

A good deal has been written about the brainwashing programs of the Chinese Communists. I have no personal knowledge of these Maoist enterprises, but my experiences during World War II convinced me that Chiang's government was then engaged in extensive efforts to brainwash large numbers of Chinese citizens.

The Generalissimo was president of the Training Institute, and it was especially dear to his heart. He frequently lectured to the students himself. Here one found the pure essence of the Kuomingtang party. Although a few "safe" foreigners had been invited to lecture to the students, we were the first Americans to be regularly employed as instructors at the institute.

Every candidate for every important civil service post in the National Government of China in 1944 was required to graduate from the National Central Political Training Institute. Every man or woman who aspired to go abroad to study in a foreign university must first pass through the institute. The motto of the institute was "One Nation, One Party, One Leader, No Opposition Either within or without the Party." Such indoctrination, in my estimation, amounts to brainwashing.

If one thought the right thoughts, said the right things, and toadied to the right people, one might attain one's personal ambition. If one was independent in mind and speech, and inclined to follow one's conscience, the party discovered this in the institute, and one could be shunted into a dark corner to rot. Wise men and women stifled their consciences, said "yes" to the proper people at the proper time, and prospered. This was democracy in

Chungking in 1944. In retrospect, it looks similar to democracy in any country controlled by Communists in the
1970s.

But no American should be too harsh in his political
judgments on either Taipei or Peking. Every people has a
right to its own political institutions. American democracy
is different from any other form of government. It evolved
to suit specific needs of the American people. The American type of democracy is good for us, but we have no right
to assume that others should imitate America. For at least
fifty years we have judged the peoples of Asia in terms of
how American they are. We have promoted American solutions for Asian problems. This idiocy has led us from
one disaster to another, culminating in Vietnam.

We give lip service to self-determination, but we assume that through the process of free political choice
people of other cultures will adopt American institutions
and solutions. This seldom happens. If another people
decides it wants a system of government which is unlike
ours, we have no right to interfere. Our failure to build a
foreign policy on this foundation has frequently made our
policy during this century a menace to some of our neighbors and sometimes has endangered the best interests of
the American people.

Both Chiang Kai-shek and Mao Tse-tung were and
are authoritarian. They both advocate that their people be
disciplined into a political and social mold of their choosing. They may both be right since the Chinese people have
been described by their own philosophers as a heap of
sand. They are one of the most individualistic peoples in
the world. Their social and political system worked as
long as China was not subject to intense international

competition. When Chiang came into power, China had been going downhill for a century. The country was a semicolony struggling to preserve some measure of national self-respect and independence.

The chief reason for China's continued existence as a political entity had been the American Open Door policy. For reasons which may not have been entirely disinterested, in 1899 the American secretary of state, John Hay, insisted that all nations should have equal access to China's markets and raw materials, and that China should be encouraged to attain political stability and independence. This policy protected China from partition until the Japanese attack in 1937.

During this period, knowledgeable Chinese looked to us as their avowed protector. The prestige created by our national policy was augmented by the activities of missionaries and relief agencies. Most American businessmen in China also enhanced our standing by comparatively fair dealing and democratic personnel practices. It was generally pleasant to be an American in China before 1937.

Our own war with Japan was largely the result of the abrogation of the Open Door policy by Japan when she attacked China. A powerful and energetic Japan insisted that she was entitled to special rights and privileges in China. Japan also feared China would become a serious rival if the rapid progress of 1927 to 1937 continued.

The Kuomingtang, first under Sun Yat-sen, and later under Chiang, faced the necessity of rebuilding China in a world full of intense nationalism. Quite properly, they were not willing to rely exclusively on

American friendship; there is a story that Sun Yat-sen asked Lenin what China should do. Lenin said that China should rely on herself, on her own people for her regeneration, because no other nation on earth would help China to become a first-rank power. The party of Sun Yat-sen became in the narrow sense a Nationalist party.

After Chiang's defeat by the Japanese in eastern China, the National Central Political Training Institute at Chungking was created to speed the process of remaking China according to Kuomingtang ideas. There has been a strong tendency on the part of American friends of China to ignore the nature of these ideas. Americans prefer to believe what they want to believe. This is a basic cause of successive American defeats in East Asia for many years.

The principal sources of inspiration of the Chinese Nationalist revolution are, first, the lectures of Sun Yat-sen, especially his *Will* (a brief statement of political principles commonly recited aloud at school and college convocations, and at many public gatherings), and, secondly, the utterances of Chiang Kai-shek, summed up in his book. Sun Yat-sen's *Will* and other papers are available in American libraries. The Chiang book did not officially become available to Americans until after World War II because prudent Kuomingtang chiefs feared it might be shocking to American sensibilities.

Here are a few choice items from the Nationalist Creed as I saw it being taught in the National Central Political Training Institute in 1944:

> *Chiang Kai-shek is our Leader and we owe him absolute obedience.*

>*There can be no opposition whatsoever to the Generalissimo and his government.*
>
>*The Chinese are the only racially pure people in the world, a chosen people who in recent years, through no fault of their own, have fallen on evil times.*
>
>*The evils which China has suffered are the gift of the West to China.*
>
>*Western civilization is fundamentally inferior to that of China because the Chinese possess superior spiritual values unknown in the materialistic West.*
>
>*The Chinese people must unite in creating a new nation "for, of, and by the people."*
>
>*All barriers to unity must be destroyed.*
>
>*When the Chinese nation is once again strong, she will eliminate Western influences, and will demand the return of her ancient territories.*

These territories, as shown on Nationalist maps, include much of Siberia, Central Asia, Southeast Asia, Korea, Japan, and parts of India. It is reported that Mao shares with Chiang a determination to add these areas to China.

Both Nationalist and Communist Chinese are motivated by strong imperialistic ambitions. Sun Yat-sen, Chiang, and Mao agree that all the territory in Asia that ever belonged to China, and all the territory in which there is a preponderance of Chinese people should be incorporated into a new China. Some definitions claim all areas which in centuries past sent tribute to the Chinese emperor must be included.

These claims have been committed to paper for many years, and are familiar to Americans who make it their business to know such things. It is comforting for Americans to believe that this rabid nationalism is nothing but a collection of slogans designed to bring together the loose sand of the people of China and mold them into a block of granite. But Chinese and Americans both have a tendency to believe political slogans.

It was inevitable that Chinese and Japanese ambitions collide; they may collide again. The Japanese taught their people that it was the sacred duty of Japan to bring all the world under one roof; a prelude was the creation of a greater East Asia Co-Prosperity Sphere, meaning a Japanese Empire in East Asia. The result to Japan was a military disaster. But the Chinas of both Chiang and Mao seem to follow the same intellectual imperialistic path blazed by the Samurai. Only the terminology is different.

I came to admire General "Vinegar Joe" Stilwell. The Stilwell policy of not taking sides in domestic policies in China was fundamentally sound. The abrogation of this policy, and the adoption of one of intervention on the side of the Nationalists in the end proved to be a disaster to the American people.

In 1945 I wrote, "Our stake in Asia is very great. The peace of the world, possibly the continued existence of the world we know, depends on the orderly and peaceful development of the peoples of Asia. It has become necessary for America to know what China really intends to do, what the Chinese Nationalist government is really like. We have no desire to impose anything on the Chinese, or any other people. It is our right to know whether the Chinese will be likewise bound to such a code." This statement remains correct.

While teaching at the institute, we lived some distance from it. Every morning we walked up the long, generally muddy hill to meet our classes. There was usually someone shadowing us. We could think of no good reason why four American officers, friends and allies of China, engaged in helping to train interpreter officers, should be shadowed. At first it made us angry, but soon the situation became amusing.

We invented games to play with the poor soul who had to follow us. He liked to listen to our conversation hoping to pick up treasonable tidbits. When we felt cooperative, we would stay together in a group. Then he would stroll a few paces back of us and listen to what we said. On these occasions we were careful to utter some opinions that he would feel justified in reporting to his superiors. Sometimes we outdid ourselves for his benefit.

When we felt energetic, we would suddenly stretch our longer legs and double our speed. He would soon be purple in the face. Then we would stop to admire the scenery, and he would stop, too, to catch his breath. Then we would string out in a long line perhaps fifty yards apart. That was the cruelest blow of all, because he could not successfully shadow all four of us, and there were no conversations to report.

When we arrived at the institute, we would go to our respective classes. We had understood that the school had no other purpose than the training of interpreters, and that English would be the sole subject taught. We soon discovered that English was a secondary consideration, that politics came first. Since a majority of the boys knew little English, and some none at all, it was obvious that in six weeks time it would not be possible to make them adequate interpreters.

We taught in various classrooms and mess halls. I particularly enjoyed two mess halls where there were a number of holes in the stone foundations. Never have I seen rats as big as those which attended my lectures. They were ignored by the students, and wandered around as tame as cats, but swifter and more sinister. There was a huge patriarch who would sometimes stop, lean against the wall, and listen to me. I flattered myself that he had a desire for learning until I noticed that he let other smaller rats forage for him on the dirt floor. When another rat found a choice morsel, the big fellow would descend on him, give him a beating, and make off with the prize. About twice in each lecture some small rat would thus be robbed to the accompaniment of shrill screams.

Our students were pleasant and courteous to me. They seemed to fit three categories. The first consisted of boys who knew some English and were willing to make a go of it, learn military discipline, and serve their country and the American army. Another type was clever and smooth, and pretended to know no English because he resented the whole program. Then there were the great majority who did not know English, and could not possibly learn it in six weeks. They resented the halting of their college careers. They liked us personally, but they knew and we knew that it had been a mistake to conscript them.

We assumed that it was the desire of the official in charge of the training program that the interpreters should be able to interpret. We told him a majority of the boys would be of no value whatever as interpreters.

We suggested that only those who knew English should be retained, and that the rest should be sent back to school, to make good engineers, lawyers, doctors, and so on, for China. He said this was impossible. A very exalted man had decreed that these male college seniors be drafted as interpreters, and he would lose face if the program was changed. Furthermore, this great man had been informed that all these young men were expert in the English language. He must not know that someone had lied to him.

This controversy went on and on. There were in China thirteen American-supported colleges and universities. The standards in these institutions were generally high. The English taught was the best in China. Hundreds of students from these schools had already volunteered for service with the American forces. Then the volunteering had been mysteriously forbidden. There remained in these institutions a pool of English-speaking boys almost large enough to take care of the immediate needs of the army for interpreters.

We pressed for the drafting of these boys. We were met with evasions. After weeks of intermittent argument, a prominent official said, "Do you really want to know why we won't draft the boys from the Christian colleges? I'll tell you. It is because they have been too much in contact with Americans, and have heard too much about democracy."

One dull, gray morning the Generalissimo inspected the center. For hours before he arrived, the place was excited and uneasy. The main road from the gate to the auditorium was heavily guarded by young peasant soldiers in their best uniforms.

The moment arrived. The Generalissimo stepped

from his limousine at the gate. He was surrounded by a galaxy of generals. He paced out in front of the group. Alone, with a quick nervous stride, he walked down the mountain. About five paces behind him was the first of the attendant generals. All walked with stiff precision.

The Generalissimo looked to neither side. He was a slim vigorous figure, an incarnation of the military spirit. His height was accentuated by a cape which was held together by a clasp on his chest. The little peasant guards saluted with exaggerated precision as the cortege passed. They were obviously frightened. They dare do nothing wrong. Like a man driven by some overwhelming inner compulsion, the Generalissimo swept by on his solitary course.

One makes so many good friends in China. There were a number of teachers brought in from universities, banks, churches, and homes to help train the interpreters. They were all Chinese with superior educations, many of them graduates of famous American universities. We met them frequently at lunch.

One of my new friends, Mr. Chen, the inspiration for this book, was a slender, elderly gentleman, intelligent and good humored. We generally avoided private conversations at the institute. Mr. Chen knew I was much interested in Chinese monasteries and offered to guide me to one a short distance away in the hills.

One afternoon we started out—Mr. Chen, another American, and myself. After an hour of keeping up with the fast-swinging pace set by the old man, I began to inquire when we would reach the monastery. Mr. Chen was indefinite. With much probing, I discovered that walking was his hobby, that he understood all Americans ride in cars and jeeps, and that he was out to prove that he, at the age of sixty, was a better man than two American officers.

We had walked without pause for ten miles, when we reached a monastery known as Flower Cliff. It was located in a shallow, rock-walled valley, a pleasant spot. It was one of the few monasteries in that part of China, according to Mr. Chen, which had not at some point in history been looted by troops. During past wars, soldiers frequently were billeted in monasteries, and when they left there was seldom anything left behind worth carrying away.

Flower Cliff had a fine garden where the flowers were already in bloom. There were also some excellent mosaics, and various treasures accumulated through the years. But it was too late in the afternoon for a leisurely inspection. Before we got back all three of us were tired out. The other American found a horse and said to hell with it, he would ride and let me uphold American honor. Chen and I were both exhausted before we reached Chungking. I had the advantage because he had a mile farther to walk before he got home.

When he saw his wife she said, "Where on earth have you been all this time? Do you want supper?"

He answered, "Never mind where I have been and I don't want supper. I'm going to bed." He did, and slept fourteen hours; so he told me the next day.

Our relations with the students and with the other staff members were always pleasant. I found several old friends on the institute staff. One was a former student whom I had regarded as close to being a moron. He had failed the same course six consecutive times at the

University of Nanking. When I pressed for his dismissal from the university, in accordance with the published regulations, I was informed that this was impossible because his party connections were too strong. Here he was at the institute, teaching the political principles of the party.

The American instructors continued to insist that for a man to be an interpreter it was necessary to know English. We protested to both the Chinese and American authorities that the majority of these students could never be employed as interpreters. The Chinese informed the Americans that we were wrong, that these men all knew English. We were ordered to give them all a careful examination.

There were about eight hundred and fifty college men in our classes in the institute. Every one was given a personal interview and graded accordingly. Those who could speak English generally were glad to do so and spoke freely. Several told me they did not think much of the institute because it was a Fascist institution.

We finally certified that about one hundred were qualified to receive an opportunity to act as interpreters for the American forces. Of these, fifty actually had adequate English, and the others might learn. It was obvious to us that these men were recruited to act primarily as spies on the activities of Americans in China. We could see no reason why American officers should be required to train people to spy on them.

The Chinese authorities graduated them all as interpreters and made a formal complaint against us to American headquarters in Chungking. The four American officers at the National Central Political Training

Institute were accused of activities inimical to Sino-American relations. We were removed by our superiors.

The final act of the comedy was a commencement ceremony when the boys all received certificates. Students and instructors stood at attention in the auditorium. The *Will* of Sun Yat-sen was read. There was a minute of silence, then all the Chinese bowed three times reverently to the portrait of Dr. Sun.

After standing for about forty minutes there was a stir, and Ho Ying-ching, minister of war, entered the hall. He was elegantly dressed, and had arrived in a limousine, but he solemnly informed the young men before him that as a proof of the democracy in China, they as interpreters would receive the same munificent salary he received as minister of war. No one dared smile. Finally there were three cheers, a Fascist salute, and it was over.

Our service in the National Central Political Training Institute for the first time put me in touch with what was actually going on in the Kuomingtang. What I saw I did not like; and I don't like it now. Fascism and communism are different sides of the same coin.

3 SACO and XYZ

When I first encountered Mr. Chen, American involvement with the Chiang regime in China seemed to me chaotic. There was considerable mutual recrimination; the military and economic alliances were not working effectively; however, there was a determination on the American side to continue to support a weak, corrupt regime which was rapidly losing popular support.

In China, in 1944 and 1945, two of the more important Sino-American joint projects were known as SACO and the XYZ plan. The initials SACO stood for Sino-American Cooperative Organization. General Tai Li and the secret societies, plus Commodore Miles's navy detachment, plus OSS in China constituted SACO. In my opinion, from the standpoint of American interests, SACO was a disaster. This operation will be discussed in detail later. The second major joint enterprise, the once highly secret XYZ project, was also a disaster.

The primary mission of all American forces in China and elsewhere in the Pacific area was the defeat of Japan. In order to ensure this defeat it was necessary to keep China in the war. China represented the only continental base from which we could hit the Japanese Empire. There were strong pro-Japanese elements in Chungking. Before Pearl Harbor, actual warfare between Japanese and Nationalist Chinese forces had practically ceased. Thus both a military and diplomatic problem was involved in our relations with the Chungking government.

General Stilwell was sent to China because he had spent many years in that country, spoke the language, and supposedly liked the people. He seemed an ideal choice for this command. He had done an excellent job in

Burma, and when he went to China it was with high
hopes of being able to make a major contribution to the
defeat of Japan. He was chief of staff to Chiang Kai-shek
and commander in chief of all American forces in the
China-Burma-India theater.

There were three main strategic aspects of the war
in this theater. One was supply. This involved the development of air transport over the Hump, and this was a
brilliant achievement of the American army air force.

The second strategic concept involved establishing
and maintaining an extensive and potent clandestine
operation near and behind the Japanese lines, with many
functions. These included guerrilla warfare to keep the
Japanese off balance; extensive networks of independent
intelligence agencies; weather observers to advise our
aircraft; attempts to disseminate information favorable
to the allies; rescue teams for American airmen shot
down in dangerous areas; and other activities essential
to the successful prosecution of the war.

Immense amounts of supplies were necessary to
support both the secret and the open wars against Japan.
The latter included the Fourteenth Air Force, together
with the Chinese-American Composite Wing, and later
the Twentieth Bomber Command and the Tenth Air
Force, and some activities of the Sino-American Cooperative Organization. But air power could not occupy territory; it was also necessary that ground forces be available. Thus the third strategic concept involved the
creation of a powerful new Chinese army.

The American strategy had two military objectives.
The first involved recapture of Burma and the reopening
of the Burma Road so that Chinese armies could be

adequately supplied; heavy tanks and artillery could not be carried by air. Once the first objective was achieved, the second could be undertaken; this would involve the defeat of the Japanese imperial army on the Asiatic mainland.

General Stilwell was the father of these basic strategic concepts. Three great Chinese armies were to be trained and equipped by Americans. These forces would cooperate with American forces later to be landed on the China coast to drive the Japanese out of their Greater East Asia.

At the time of Pearl Harbor, there were supposed to be about three hundred undermanned and poorly equipped divisions in the Chinese army. Out of these, Chiang agreed to supply Stilwell with men for three great task forces.

X-Force was to be based in Burma and Assam and would consist of about twenty divisions. It would include men who had retreated from Burma to India with Stilwell, reinforced by new men to be flown over the Hump. Very few reinforcements appeared. Stilwell finally was given two ragged divisions to use in the reconquest of North Burma from Assam. These men were trained near Ramgarh and became the elite divisions of the Chinese army. With little or no support from the Chinese, they did on occasion defeat the Japanese and in the process suffered heavy casualties.

Y-Force was to consist of about twenty divisions with headquarters in Kunming. They were expected to drive west across the Salween to join X-Force. After that, both forces were to wheel eastward and join Z-Force, centered around Kweilin, and similar in size to Y-Force,

Legend:

⊙ Stilwell's bases
   Main OSS bases
   Main U.S. air bases
■ Supply
□ 14th Air Force
▨ 21st Bomber Command
XYZ X-Y-Z forces
   Approximate area controlled
   by the Japanese
   Spring 1944
   Winter 1944-1945
   Approximate area of Chinese-Communist
   party headquarters
   The Hump

C.C. Weiss
S.I.U. Cartographic Laboratory

Source used for spelling of Chinese place names is
Hammond World Atlas (Maplewood, N.J.: Hammond, Inc., 1967).

for a drive to the coast to meet American landing parties. The final step would be a joint Sino-American drive north into Manchuria, the great Japanese mainland base.

Stilwell's strategy did not work for several reasons. The chief reason was the unwillingness of the Chinese to make it work. The A-bomb forced the Japanese to surrender before a major land campaign was launched, but Japan might have surrendered even earlier if the Chinese high command had lived up to its commitments.

It was apparent that there were many prominent Chinese who did not want America to win the war or at least to win it too quickly. That would give America too much power, make America and American ideals too popular with the oppressed masses in China. Also, many high Chinese officials were making too much money from their trade with the enemy to be happy about giving it up. The black market was making millionaires of many in power, and this would end with victory. As a whole, the Chinese army took all that it could get from the Americans and gave little in return.

Japanese psychological warfare might have had something to do with it. The nature of the military agreement between Chungking and Washington made it vulnerable to Japanese propaganda attacks. Americans were supposed to be teachers and helpers, and Chinese to be fighters in the X, Y, and Z Forces. This agreement was made at the insistence of the Chinese government. Day after day, the Japanese radio bombarded the Chinese army with derision for offering itself as cannon fodder for America.

General Stilwell proved to have many human weaknesses, but he did possess a special quality rare among generals, a certain political sense. He defined American objectives in Asia in this way: Our primary objective in China was the defeat of Japan; secondly, Americans in his command were to keep out of local politics; finally, America should not be permitted to become involved in any postwar Asian commitments. He lost on the last two points.

The general was considered by many members of his command as so fond of the Chinese that he was known in some army quarters as a "chink-lover." He was also a wary guardian of American interests. He objected strongly to the hoarding of American war supplies by the Chinese army and to its reluctance to fulfill its obligations.

Unfortunately, Stilwell was not supported by some of his associates. Among those who did not support him was General Hurley who as ambassador insisted on a blind approval of the Generalissimo and all his works. Also, Commodore Milton Miles, the key American naval figure in China, seemed to consider himself independent of the American supreme commander and insisted on supporting his good friend General Tai Li.

The open war in China never got far beyond the planning stage, but the secret one was an ugly reality. There were many reasons why the secret war was necessary; it might have been an important factor in the defeat of Japan if it had not been for Tai Li's double-dealing.

One of the first objectives of the secret war was a reliable intelligence net behind and near the Japanese lines. Certain cities, such as Shanghai, Peking, Hankow, Tientsin, Hongkong, and Canton, with many smaller Japanese-held centers, were important Japanese bases.

The American army could have made great use of a net of trained and reliable agents living in these areas.

There were many Chinese men and women who did superb work for the Americans as spies in Japanese territory in spite of Tai Li. Here is a characteristic story. There was an apparently half-witted Chinese who lived near certain switchyards on one of China's principal railroads. He seemed harmless, so the Japanese let him wander as he pleased. He made a habit of strolling in the neighborhood of Japanese military trains.

When the Japanese were preparing for their last Central China offensive, this rail yard was an important base. At one time there were several hundred freight cars there and a number of locomotives. They were well camouflaged so the Japanese did not fear attack by the Fourteenth Air Force. Their consternation was great when a large flight of American planes appeared and proceeded to blast the cars and locomotives. The damage was terrific. Obviously something had gone wrong.

A lot of people were rounded up and tortured to make them confess that they had acted as spies for the Americans. Among them was our half-wit. He was horribly beaten, but when he told nothing the Japanese let him go. Thereupon he reported the whole affair to the Americans over a secret radio and continued to be a spy. He was moved to another location because it would be too much of a coincidence if another Japanese concentration was hit after he had been snooping around. His work was typical of that done by many anti-Japanese Chinese for the American forces. And usually such work was done out of patriotism only, for the compensation was small.

There were also brave Americans who lived for months in the shadow of the Japanese, organizing spy rings, and personally reporting on the activities of the Japanese and the puppet armies. One such was Captain John Birch, a young man who had been a Baptist missionary in China before the war. He joined the OSS and became one of its key men in what was called the Anhwei pocket, a region north of the Yangtze in Central China where the Japanese had not penetrated the mountains and the marshes. Birch spoke Mandarin extremely well and had lived among the Chinese so long he seemed in his thinking almost as much Chinese as American. He served through the war in his exposed position with little recognition from his American superiors; he was killed by the Communists under circumstances which will be discussed in a later chapter.

Another American whose name I cannot recall was a private who, for many months, was stationed as a solitary lookout near Changsha. He lived in a temple on a hill above an arm of Tungting Lake. One day he saw a fleet of about thirty Japanese shallow draft transports heading in his direction. He estimated that they contained a total of about nine thousand men and horses, a whole Japanese cavalry division. He had a small, agent's radio and immediately got in touch with the Fourteenth Air Force. For some nine hours, he ground out the message, in the clear, that a Japanese cavalry division was disembarking on the shore of the lake in front of him. He kept it up all through the attack because he wanted to be able to guide successive waves of American planes. In the end the division withdrew with a few hundred survivors. Then he settled down to wait for some more excitement.

Another function of the secret war and its partici-
pants on the Chinese-American side was the rescue of
stranded American airmen and other allied personnel
trying to escape from the Japanese. The Air Ground Aid
Service, AGAS for short, did a remarkably efficient job
in organizing escape routes for such people. This was a
generally successful joint American and Chinese enterprise.

AGAS deserves a great deal of credit. It was particularly successful in Communist territory. It reported that
the Communists never accepted any reward for the
rescue of American personnel. An American pilot who
hid for several months in the barren Northwest told me
he was wonderfully cared for by the poverty-stricken
people. In Nationalist territory, it was frequently necessary to pay large sums to cover "expenses."

During the whole war in the Pacific, up to V-J Day,
it was assumed that someday there would be a major
American landing somewhere on the China coast. This
involved a great deal of planning and preparation, and
many Americans lived long under difficult circumstances
as they explored the harbors and islands off the coast
and mapped routes into the interior. Their sacrifices
were largely wasted.

Finally, one of the most important objectives of our
secret war was the organization, training, equipping, and
operation of guerrilla bands. In China, World War II
was fought in a primitive manner. There were millions
of men available who hated the Japanese and professed
to be our friends. By organizing them as guerrillas the
Japanese could be kept constantly on the alert, and losses
could be inflicted which would be hard to replace.

Sometimes there were specific targets to be attacked,

such as the railroad bridges across the Yellow River, which were so important to the Japanese that they were each guarded by as much as a regiment of antiaircraft artillery. This concentration of guns kept the American planes flying so high that they never were able to knock the bridges out for long. These bridges had to be attacked on foot or by swimmers in the stealthy guerrilla manner, and this was done twice to my knowledge under the leadership of American OSS officers.

A well-organized and coordinated secret campaign that was able to make use of a sizeable fraction of the human and material resources available in China could have caused great damage to the Japanese and might have hastened the end of the war. That this was not done, I believe, was chiefly the fault of Tai Li, the titular leader of China's secret forces. Not only would he not permit his own organization to fight such a war, but he also placed many obstacles in the way of the Americans and other Chinese who tried to do it without his assistance.

Now we turn to another kind of war. The Sino-American Cooperative Organization originated when American officers, including Captain, later Commodore (before his promotion to Rear Admiral), Miles, went to Chungking to organize secret warfare behind the Japanese lines. For years American papers had been carrying stories of the valor and resourcefulness of the Chinese guerrillas, who supposedly had fought the Japanese to a standstill practically with their bare hands. Now these guerrillas were going to be armed, equipped, and trained by American specialists, and life was going to become dangerous for the Japanese.

When the Generalissimo was approached in the

matter, he gave the project his approval providing the nominal and actual head was a Chinese. He nominated General Tai Li to be his representative. The American co-chief was Miles. The headquarters of the new SACO was to be in Tai Li's organizational headquarters in Happy Valley, about twelve miles outside Chungking.

It looked like an ideal setup. The agreement was formally approved by the highest authorities in Washington and Chungking. On the American side, SACO was all inclusive—all American organizations doing secret work in China were to be in SACO under Tai Li's supervision. The basic reasoning was logical: China was our ally and shared our objectives; on Chinese territory the command responsibility should be Chinese. It never worked because the Chinese had their own objectives, some of them opposed to ours.

So money, men, and equipment were flown over the Hump to Happy Valley and sent out to the remote stations operated by SACO in East China. All was enthusiasm and good will. Nominally, Tai Li had some seven million men under his command, most of them members of the secret societies. Wonders were going to be performed.

Time passed and wonders failed to materialize. Washington began to ask questions. American morale in the Valley began to go down. I was one of those who believed that Tai Li did not want American secret warfare against the Japanese in China to be successful.

Here is a typical story. There were two OSS officers near one of the Yellow River bridges. They were supposed to be instructing Tai Li agents in the art of being guerrillas. Our boys were forbidden to command troops or to engage in combat. However, they got their students so enthused that they went out and blew up several piers of a nearby bridge so effectively that Japanese movements over that railroad were held up for about three months. The Japanese Changsha campaign was delayed.

Tai Li recalled both these American officers with a rebuke for usurping authority. Their group of enthusiastic students was broken up. The only logical conclusion was that Tai Li did not want either his own men or the Americans in his command to fight the Japanese.

Up to this time, Miles had been head of the entire American secret warfare enterprise in China. His command consisted of two diverse elements. There was a large navy detachment and there was a smaller OSS group.

OSS headquarters became dissatisfied with the way things were going, and General Donovan himself went to China to see what was the matter. General Donovan must have been handicapped in his dealings with Tai Li by his lack of knowledge of the Chinese people. There was always a lack of competent China-trained personnel in his immediate staff. In my opinion, OSS would have been much more successful in China if it had made better use of the China experts in the organization.

Tai Li was a past master at capitalizing on American weaknesses, chiefly wine and women. Donovan's visit was celebrated by a banquet in which much wine was drunk, with the host always poised like a hawk to take advantage of any indiscretions on the part of his guests. That was the Tai Li technique, which he sometimes used to great effect.

The issue on this occasion was the inability of OSS

to get anything done under Tai Li's domination. According to some of my friends who were present, Donovan remained cold sober. "Wild Bill" was always famous for direct and forceful speech. He said bluntly that OSS had a mission to perform and if it could not be performed in cooperation with Tai Li, then OSS would operate separately.

Tai Li flared up and said, "If OSS tries to operate outside of SACO I will kill your agents."

Donovan answered, "For every one of our agents you kill, we will kill one of your generals," and he pounded the table with his fist.

"You can't talk to me like that," shouted Tai Li.

"I am talking to you like that," said Donovan.

The two masters of intrigue suddenly calmed down and were all smiles. The OSS continued to be in SACO and was promised many things by Tai Li. But never was the OSS able to accomplish much under the leadership and supervision of Tai Li. Some of its quite substantial achievements were technically illegal since they were carried out independently of SACO.

In early 1944 American command in SACO was split, and the OSS detachment was placed under Colonel Coughlin, a very capable regular army officer. The navy contingent continued under Miles. It was expanded until the command was so large it justified Miles's promotion to rear admiral. Unfortunately, the two chief American elements in the secret war, the OSS and the navy, did not work well together.

It is no reflection on the individual Americans involved to ask what business did the American navy have on the Chinese mainland. The only visible reason at the time was that Roosevelt was a navy man, and Admiral Leahy was his close adviser. The navy wanted a piece of the action in China and the president gave the navy what it wanted. The result was a split American command in China. The highly competent navy men in SACO, from Miles on down, should have gone down to the sea in ships.

Because the navy detachment was completely under Tai Li's thumb, it received preferential treatment from the Chinese. The OSS, on the other hand, which was mainly staffed by U.S. Army personnel, insisted on the fulfillment by the Chinese of their obligations. The greater such insistence, the less Tai Li liked the OSS.

Another reason for Tai's dislike of the OSS was his evident belief that it was a complete secret service organization like his own. He did not want the OSS to become too strong in China. In many subtle ways he made it impossible for it to fulfill its mission in China. The only exception was the training functions of the OSS. He was generally willing for Chinese soldiers to learn whatever Americans could teach them. But it was not easy to put training into practice.

Once, after months of preparation and the expenditures of extravagant sums of money, an expedition set out for the coast where an intelligence net was to be set up in Shanghai. The American in charge of this program was on the Japanese blacklist and if he had been captured, things would have been particularly hard for him. He set up his headquarters in a small mountain village and sent his band of Tai Li agents off toward Shanghai.

He did not hear from them for weeks. He had uneasy visions of their having been captured by the Japanese and having died horrible deaths. There were other considerations too, for under torture they might have given away the secrets of the entire operation. Then he discovered that the whole gang was sitting in a village about fifty miles away and had been there all the time. They had various excuses but the truth was they had no intention of going to Shanghai as American spies. It was too dangerous. Furthermore, Tai Li just did not want the expedition to be a success. If he had, the fear of possible death at the hands of the Japanese would have been over-balanced by the certainty of death at the hands of Tai Li.

This story could be multiplied many times. Since Tai Li represented the Generalissimo, every effort made to dislodge him failed. He obstructed efforts by the OSS except in the area of training and equipping its own agents from beginning to end, because he was sure he could control such Chinese agents. Being much smarter than most of the Americans with whom he dealt, he hood-winked each according to his own nature. To some he was soft, to others, hard. Sometimes his own commanders made a sincere effort to help the Americans. Sometimes such commanders were mysteriously transferred or dis-appeared. The navy group, under Miles, considered Tai Li their commander and in general followed his orders scrupulously. Through this group, as we shall see, Tai Li secured large amounts of supplies and was able to consolidate his position in China.

In retrospect, I believe Tai Li was an enemy of the United States in China in World War II. I believe our support of Tai Li was a disaster. We were able to win the China war in spite of Tai Li and others like him in the Kuomingtang because we won the war at sea and on the islands of the Pacific, and because of the Bomb. If there is any lesson to be learned it is this: It is extremely dangerous to act in Asia without a complete knowledge of the facts. It is essential that American policies should be based on a thorough knowledge of the economic, social, and political realities. Unfortunately, we have consistently based our policies on ignorance and on wishful thinking. We have consistently backed the status quo, the rich and the landlords, on a continent undergoing a social and economic revolution. This has led us from one tragedy to another.

4 Tai Li and Death Valley

I first became aware of the existence of SACO when I noticed that groups of U.S. Navy men occasionally appeared on the streets of Chungking, then mysteriously disappeared. When I asked where they came from, the answer was generally ribald. Someone finally told me they belonged to Tai Li's Happy Valley. They were cloak and dagger boys. The Japanese knew all about them, but they still were a top secret as far as American and Chinese government officials were concerned.

As an American who spoke Chinese, I heard nasty stories about Tai Li's organization. Sometimes liberal professors, writers, or artists disappeared from their classrooms or homes; it was rumored that they had landed in Happy Valley, as Tai Li insisted on calling his headquarters.

My Chinese friends sometimes asked, "Why do you Americans work with a man like Tai Li? Don't you understand what he is, what he stands for? Don't you realize that he is only using you for what he can get out of you?" There was no answer to these questions. Somebody at the top had made a mistake and there was nothing for little people to do except obey orders. I had no idea that before long I would be working for Tai Li.

The secrecy which surrounded the Valley was absurd. The Japanese obviously knew what was happening there. One night, Radio Tokyo broadcast a list of the senior American officers in the Valley, with a derisive summary of their plans. Since the Americans in the Valley carefully maintained their security, there was only one possible way for the Japanese to have secured this information which was from someone in the Tai Li organization. There was abundant circumstantial evidence indicating a direct tie-up between Tai Li's organization and Japanese intelligence. Much of my time during 1944 and 1945 was spent in an effort to identify for our own intelligence people the individuals in Tai Li's Secret Military Police who were working in China and in India for the Japanese.

Because the OSS had once been under Miles and was still part of SACO, the headquarters of OSS in China were in the Valley. When I was transferred to OSS, I had no idea what the organization was or did. I knew a little more about the Valley. My education proceeded rapidly. Tai Li insisted, for reasons of security, that when a man once moved out to the Valley, he should stay there. Together with some other officers, I delayed going into the hills as long as possible. Chungking had few attractions, but it was better than prison. One reason I was personally most reluctant to go to the Valley was my connection through Mr. Chen with the middle-of-the-road dissidents who were regarded by Tai Li as mortal enemies of the Chiang regime.

One fine May morning we set out for the Valley. Spring in the Yangtze basin is beautiful. The sun peers uncertainly through the mists, and the whole earth blossoms in the warmth. Everywhere there is the fragrance of growth and the sound of running water. The car carried us over a bumpy road to the foot of a range of steep mountains. The tops of the peaks were generally bare but there was a good deal of vegetation on the slopes, including some fine pine woods. At right angles to the main range were a series of valleys, each carrying a small stream which was lined with small farms.

The car stopped at the foot of such a valley, close to the tall range—which was imposing because it rose so abruptly from the lowlands. A footpath edged by small trees led up the valley toward the mountains. Coolies grabbed our luggage, and off we started. It was like home-coming to me because the Chinese countryside was so familiar. There were the customary cuckoos calling in the thickets. Little boys were fishing for small, silvery fish in the pools, just as I had fished when I was their age.

There were guard posts at several points along the road; after passing the last of these, we ascended a flight of steep steps and there was the Valley. It was a lovely place. Tai Li had built a series of low, one-story houses on the slope ahead of us. They were connected by flagstone paths with the stone steps that are so familiar in China.

The navy and OSS had been administratively di-vorced by now and the feeling between them was not cordial. OSS had been assigned a group of new buildings in a glen below the navy establishment. The ground around the lath-and-plaster buildings had been cleared and was planted with flowers. It was a pleasant spot. There were even two fine bathrooms with all the fixtures, including two huge tubs built for giants. I gazed upon these with delight until I was informed that the plumbing didn't work and never had; it never did.

Our own mess had not yet started, so at first we ate with the navy. The mess hall was an imposing building on a stone terrace surrounded by young pine trees. It was generally cooler than any other place in the Valley be-cause the wind always seemed to hit this spot.

The mess was an unforgettable experience. The waiters were a slovenly, disagreeable crew and the food like nothing I had ever eaten before. Miles had ordered that everyone eat Chinese food as a gesture of friendship.

But the Chinese cooks tried to make the food resemble American dishes. As a result, it resembled nothing. Everyone had to use chopsticks and since most of the men present were newcomers to China, they sprayed the tables with food. It was unpleasant, and we resolved to establish our own mess as soon as possible.

For the plentiful but unappetizing fare provided in the navy mess, everyone paid two dollars per day. Here I became acquainted with a strange military and naval anomaly. The naval officers were all being paid a per diem living allowance of twelve dollars a day; the enlisted men were getting nine dollars and seventy-five cents. Both paid two dollars a day for the same food and pocketed the difference. But the army personnel in OSS were getting no allowance at all. This was only one of many evidences of interservice rivalry. I often wondered if the navy and the army were fighting the same war.

The per diem problem for OSS was later remedied; army personnel, officers and men, got an allowance of around seven dollars a day. Per diem is legally allowed when officers and men must pay excessive amounts for their food. The allowance is not supposed to exceed the cost of living. Here per diem was a racket. Since the morale was poor in this strange naval establishment on the side of a mountain in West China, this excessive allowance was one way of bolstering morale.

The same situation existed to a lesser degree in the army headquarters in Chungking. There the officers and men received a per diem which was several dollars a day in excess of their actual expenses. Soldiers in organized military units at the front whose lives were in danger received no per diem; but the boys in headquarters lived on the fat of the land and were paid extra for it. The inequities of military life were bewildering to a civilian soldier.

Before I had been in the Valley more than a day, I was taken to the interim commanding officer, General P'an Chi-wu, who was in charge during the frequent absences of General Tai Li. P'an and I were born in the same part of China and both spoke the little-known Foochow language. We were soon good friends. He talked more freely to me in his native tongue than he ever could through an interpreter.

There was another general present named Hsieh Li-kung, once a Communist, educated in a Soviet military academy in Moscow. He insisted on being called Derry by his American friends. The two generals invited me to dinner at headquarters and in the course of the meal I said something about my interest in Chinese monasteries. P'an said that he also liked them and had thought of entering one to become a monk. I asked him why. He pulled out his purse and showed me a photograph of a very attractive young girl.

"She was my fiancée," he said.

I asked why he did not marry her and he replied that she had died recently. I asked how she died and he was embarrassed. Finally he said that she died from something like a "sudden tuberculosis." Derry was listening and broke in to say in English that it would be more accurate to say that she had died of a sudden and unexpected attack of indigestion. He laughed awkwardly as he said this.

Later I discovered that P'an had been very much in love with the girl, but that Tai Li had forbidden his marriage. When P'an had insisted, the girl had suddenly died. Then P'an had asked permission to leave the organization permanently to enter a Buddhist monastery. This request was also refused, and P'an did not press the matter because he knew that Tai Li would not let him leave the secret service alive.

Tai Li was strangely jealous of the influence of women on the lives of his men. He had women in his organization, both as secret operatives and to take care of the biological needs of his men, but he objected strongly to marriage or any permanent alliances. He carried this policy to such an extreme that he insisted that our servants leave their wives behind when they came to the Valley. Tai Li had several nice villas, built in Mediterranean style, hidden in a grove of pine trees above the Valley, and the women he had there could be seen any day by the curious. P'an and Hsieh were both loyal to their master. The alternative was death. I came to know them well and liked them both.

It was common practice of the Tai Li group to throw big parties in order to make American officers drunk and encourage them to spill any secrets they might know. We were officially regarded more as possible enemies to be spied on than as allies. My turn came when Derry Hsieh gave a banquet at the Banker's Club in Chungking to which I was invited as one of the guests of honor. There were two other Americans sharing this honor, both of whom were headed for the field, meaning areas near the Japanese. The meal was superb. There were also quantities of wine, and Derry set out to make his guests drunk.

I noticed that the drinks were being poured from different kinds of bottles. I insisted that my hosts drink what was served to me. Also, I insisted that the Chinese show me the bottoms of their wine cups in the *kanpei* ceremony after each toast, which was perfectly acceptable behavior. By employing these polite devices I avoided falling into his trap. Meanwhile, Derry was drinking far more than was good for him and presently he was under the table singing "The Old Time Religion" in a nice tenor. This was his favorite song when he was drunk.

Most Chinese wine has a low alcoholic content, but in order to learn our "secrets," the Chinese sometimes served both wine and *mao tai,* or *paigarh,* which are distilled from fermented sorghum, or some other terrific potion for the soft rice wine that was customarily served at dinners. The hard liquor could be 150 proof compared to about 10 percent alcohol in the wine. The two drinks looked alike. The Chinese toasted the Americans in wine but fed the rough stuff to the Americans.

Soon the victims would be merrily drunk, their tongues would wag freely, and out came the secrets, if they knew any. It was generally a poor investment for Tai Li because I doubt if any of us knew many real secrets. However, drunkenness often led to frank statements of opinion, which in turn damaged Sino-American working relationships. In some cases, American officers may have permanently damaged their careers by expressing their honest opinion of Tai Li and his works.

During the latter part of World War II, Chinese officialdom suffered a strange obsession, the conviction that the foreigner, especially an American, was a potential enemy and must be treated with surface friendliness while all possible information was being extracted from him. This was a trait common in prewar Japan, but I had never before encountered it in China. It was one of many inconspicuous ways in which the China of Tai Li was imitating the Japan it was pretending to fight.

In the Valley, I saw several of my former students in the Interpreters' School at the Political Training Institute. They were very subdued. It was some time before I got the story of what happened to them.

A short time after their graduation, one hundred and twenty of the boys were ordered to appear at a certain place at a certain time with their belongings. They were bundled into trucks and, to their horror, soon found themselves in Tai Li's Happy Valley. From the standpoint of the average young liberal intellectual, that was a fate almost literally as bad as death. They held a meeting to try to find a way out.

The next day a committee of twelve succeeded in eluding the guards and got back to Chungking. There they called in a body on Chen Li-fu, the minister of education, demanding "protection" from Tai Li. They were turned away with soft words, were put in another truck, and taken back to the hills. They were thoroughly frightened by now.

Soon the whole detachment was called together for a meeting. Tai Li himself appeared before them. He smote himself upon the breast. "See! Here is the Monster. Here is Tai Li. Is he not a man like yourselves?" Then he pulled all the stops and gave the boys a pep talk. Somehow they were unable to work up much enthusiasm. In the end Tai Li said, "I understand some of you fellows don't want to work for me. I am very sorry. But I never force a man to work for me. You may go. You are free as the wind. But when you go, I will have a little farewell gift for you:

thirty-six dollars." Thirty-six inflated dollars was the price of a bullet. The boys decided to stay.

My first job in OSS had to do with psychological warfare. In OSS jargon our job was known as MO, short for Morale Operations. Our function was to create propaganda, spread it among the Japanese troops, and hasten the decay of their fighting spirit. It was hard to persuade the average shooting soldier that this wasn't a waste of time, yet psychological warfare was a major weapon on both sides in World War II. Our output was called black propaganda because the American origin was hidden. The Office of War Information produced and disseminated through the Voice of America and other news media the white propaganda of official American policy. We anticipated no difficulties in persuading Tai Li's outfit to help us in our job. Chinese are expert at propaganda. I was enthusiastic about the possibilities when we went to the Valley.

We never accomplished anything except to spend American money. It took real talent to be as uncooperative as were Tai Li and his aides. It was like trying to fight a ghost. We knew the opposition was there, but we could never see it. Never were we permitted to accomplish anything while part of Tai Li's Secret Military Police. The only exception to this record of failure was when some of us succeeded in getting into the field, far away from Tai Li's headquarters. There it was sometimes possible to get something accomplished.

We needed Chinese agents. These were promised to us every time we asked for them. Weeks passed and we got impatient. The agents will be with you on such and such a date, we would be told. But when the great day came, there were no agents, just new excuses. Once when the pressure on them got too strong, Tai Li's organization did produce a prospective agent to work in an important area behind the Japanese lines.

The man was duly trained and was provided with costly American equipment. We were told that he would need a large amount of money so he got it. Everyone was happy. There were speeches and loud expressions of admiration for the Sino-American Cooperative Organization as we launched this frail craft on its mission. We never heard from this man again. There was no evidence that he ever reached his destination. He just faded away with a large amount of American money and equipment in his possession, together with the "secrets," such as they were, of our plans and program.

One of our worst difficulties was transportation. We lived about a dozen miles outside Chungking. Army headquarters were there and most of us had daily business to transact in the city. Tai Li was supposed to provide us with transportation. This consisted of one broken-down LaSalle driven by an evil but amusing old fellow who shamelessly eavesdropped on us and was more of a spy than a chauffeur.

I came to know this old scoundrel well. He was particularly close to Tai Li, having driven him out of Nanking when the Japanese were close on his heels. His loyalty to the general was absolute. He knew plenty of English, and I would watch him tasting the conversation around him when there were men in the car who insisted on airing their opinions in English. Sometimes I had more or less secret missions in town. He would park the car at my request, then would follow me as I walked through the alleys to my destination. On the way back I would meet him and he would grin impudently.

The LaSalle frequently broke down. Then we were stranded. There was a car park not far away with about a thousand new trucks in it, but we could never get one. Sometimes we would elect one of ourselves to walk all the way into Chungking with the mail bag in order to be sure that our confidential reports were not tampered with. We were not treated as friends and allies. It was humiliating.

The climate in the Valley was appalling, which was one reason we called it Death Valley. During one period of twenty-eight consecutive days, our thermometer registered a maximum of at least one hundred and five degrees every day, and the nights seldom cooled down to ninety. We had no sheets and slept on GI blankets, so we were covered with prickly heat. The humidity was very high. Between the almost complete frustration, the heat, and the lack of recreation, it was remarkable that the men held up as well as they did.

All armies drink and Americans often drink too much, especially when conditions are intolerable. There was an especially bad time when everything had gone wrong. Tai Li had broken one promise after another. Washington refused to recognize the situation we faced. We received a steady stream of airy letters full of gentle persiflage and good advice and we-are-all-with-you stuff. We were fed up.

One of the younger boys was married and was always talking about his wife and new baby. He received a letter from his wife telling him of the death of his baby. When the child suddenly got sick, she had not been able to get a doctor. All day the bereaved father walked around stiff as a guardsman on parade.

One of the men had been in Chungking and made a discovery: a White Russian making gin in a private laboratory. He had a precious bottle of London Dry which he kept by his side with which he compared each batch of his own product. His gin was practically indistinguishable from the genuine article.

The officer brought home a five-gallon jar of good gin and soon we were drinking together on our terrace. Derry Hsieh came along with his latest concubine, a pretty little girl with abnormally short skirts slit to the thigh. And soon Derry was singing in his high tenor "The Old Time Religion is Good Enough for Me!"

I went to bed but the party went on and on. The young father had started out by being rather quiet, then he began to be talkative. Everyone tried to help him to forget what was on his mind. He became unsteady and disappeared from the terrace.

Suddenly there was a pistol shot just behind the men grouped around the remains of the gin. They turned to see the boy wavering in the moonlight with a .32 in his hand. His shot had skimmed above the head of another officer, who quietly said, "Mind if I look at that gun?" and took it from him. Then they led him to bed where he broke down and wept for hours. The next day most of the men had hangovers, but morale was better and stayed that way for some time. The mild orgy had cleared the atmosphere as the occasional electric storms cleared the air above the Valley.

For months Tai Li was only a legend to me. He was off on some kind of tour and we dealt with his executive, my friend P'an. Then the great man suddenly returned. The villas among the pines were full of light and women's laughter and were guarded by trigger-happy gunmen.

He came down into our part of the Valley one evening to supervise the laying of the foundation of a new building. He was a handsome, slender man with tiny, beautiful hands. He walked as if he had a ramrod for a spine. He had a strange, long stride like the exaggerated stride of the hero in a Chinese theater. He had a sharp, appraising eye which seemed to take in a man's features and his character for future reference.

Tai Li impressed me as brilliant, imaginative, ruthless, and unscrupulous. He was the Himmler of Nationalist China. He was the enemy of almost every ideal of American democracy. He tried to unify China under Chiang by enforcing iron control. He was cold, hard, crafty, and brutal. He was also much smarter than most of the Americans in his Valley. He took those who worked for him in SACO for a long, one-way ride.

Shortly after Tai Li's visit, we had a visitation of another kind. There were a few wolves on the mountains around the Valley, but otherwise there was a general lack of wild life. We had been specifically assured that there were no dangerous snakes in that part of China. One night I was watching a Chinese enlisted man carry a load of water along the stone terrace in front of our mess hall. He gave a hoarse shout, dropped his carrying-pole, and grabbed a stick with which he slashed at something on the ground. Then he began to dance on one foot while he held the other with his hands.

I ran over and found he had been bitten on the top of his foot by a small viper, which he had subsequently killed. I half-carried him into the mess hall where I put him on a spare bed and called for help. In a few minutes one of our men was administering first aid. I had called Tai Li's office to ask for a sedan chair and coolies to carry the man to the navy infirmary; I also had called the naval infirmary to ask advice from the very capable head surgeon. The snake I put in a bottle for future reference.

This young soldier was entitled to medical care under Chinese law; yet the central office showed a complete lack of interest in his fate. I explained in both English and Chinese that he had been bitten by a poisonous snake, that it was necessary for him to have medical care immediately, that the Americans would take care of him, but that he could not walk up the steep mountain path to the infirmary.

Yes, yes, it was all understood, and the office would send a chair immediately to care for the man. But the chair did not come. The man was in considerable pain. I looked at the snake and found it matched the description of the Russel's Viper of India, which is very poisonous.

The Navy infirmary sent down a contingent of men, led by the chief surgeon, a captain in the regular navy. The captain ordered his men to carry the boy to the infirmary. They did it gladly. So the coolie-soldier was put on a cot in the immaculate infirmary, and all night Americans worked on him, giving him injections of antivenom and plasma.

In a few days he was able to walk around on a crutch, and before long he was back at his work. The Chinese enlisted men in the Valley walked around talking about this wonder. The Americans had actually treated the man as if he was one of their own; they had given him medicine worth more than a hundred dollars in American money. It was wonderful. Americans were wonderful. But we heard nothing from Tai Li's headquarters for some time until there arrived a queer, embarrassed note thanking the Americans for their care of this soldier.

I took the carcass of the snake to a herpetologist at a university situated a few miles away on the plateau on top of the mountain. He returned it with the notation that it was a Russel's Viper and that to his knowledge such a snake had never before been reported in Szechwan. A few days later there was a housecleaning in our rooms and another viper was found coiled around a post of our commanding officer's bed.

Happy Valley actually consisted of three parallel valleys. We were in the center. North of us was a smaller valley, and in it was a grim prison about which unpleasant stories were told. The larger valley to the south contained various residences and schools, including a large establishment in which Tai Li agents were being trained by representatives of the American FBI, or so we were told. I never met any American who admitted he represented the FBI.

The navy group under Miles (then a commodore) played Tai Li's game. They gave Tai Li what he wanted and did not ask too many questions. Tai Li liked them and they received generally favorable treatment. At this time, the navy group was training about a thousand men a month for Tai Li. Month after month the training continued, and Tai Li agents went out from the Valley wearing American uniforms, carrying American weapons, driving American vehicles.

The excuse given in Washington was that these men were guerrillas who were being trained to fight the Japanese. I never saw any evidence to confirm the idea that any of these thousands of men ever fought the Japanese. Tai Li and his friends used American-trained agents to strengthen their hold on Nationalist China and to prepare for the coming struggle against the Communists.

Commodore Miles was honorably living up to the letter of the SACO agreement and believed the reports that Tai Li gave him concerning what was being accomplished in the field. This is apparent if one reads his book, *A Different Kind of War*. And probably some of the success stories reported to Miles were true.

OSS followed a different policy: it regarded itself as exclusively an American agency fighting America's war. Tai Li feared OSS, tried to keep it under close surveillance. In spite of the opposition of Tai Li and of Miles, OSS turned out a very creditable body of solid accomplishment in the China theater.

After Commodore Miles ceased to be acting head of OSS in China, it was hard to believe that SACO and OSS were fighting the same war. The navy in SACO fed high on the hog and OSS nearly starved. For example, SACO was allocated one hundred and fifty tons of supplies monthly to be carried from India to China over the Hump. The use of this tonnage was allocated by Tai Li and Miles. During one period of three months in the summer of 1944, when four hundred and fifty tons came over the mountains for SACO, OSS received of this amount only ten pounds. It was necessary for us to scour the shops of Chungking for paper on which to write fatuous reports for Washington, which we sent in salvaged envelopes.

There were few visible evidences of the nature of the Tai Li organization. Except for the complete futility of our lives, we lived fairly well and had no reason to complain. I was shocked out of my personal apathy one bright summer night when I could not sleep owing to the heat. There was a light north breeze. It carried over the hill from the prison, hour after hour, the terrible screams of a woman being tortured.

The next night I was exhausted and thought I would sleep in spite of the heat. But again the soft breeze bore terrifying, subhuman screams. There was no escaping the reality represented by these sounds. One could only swear to tell the story of the Valley and of Tai Li where it would do some good.

But it did no good. Report after report was sent to Washington and ignored. It became an obsession of the handful of us in the Valley that something must be done to release OSS from the Tai Li control so that it could fulfill its mission. There was no response at all from Washington. Tai Li treated us with poorly concealed contempt.

All of this time I was, in effect, a triple agent. I was an American army officer assigned to OSS, which had detailed me to Tai Li's Secret Military Police. With the approval of my OSS colonel, I worked through Mr. Chen with the secret societies, which were now dedicated to overthrowing Chiang Kai-shek and Tai Li.

5 The Royal City

OSS in Death Valley decided to make a last try to work with Tai Li. It would be a test case. Everything would be carefully planned and documented. If this project failed, if he refused to permit us to go ahead, if obstacles were put in our way, we thought we would have evidence we could use in Washington against working under the SACO agreement. If we accomplished our mission after such careful preparation, this might indicate that the fault lay on our side. We would have a successful precedent for future operations.

The nature of this test project is immaterial. It necessitated my going to Chengtu to make certain plans; the significance of the enterprise lay in its bearing on the feasibility of working with Tai Li under any circumstances. I was a messenger from OSS to the Twentieth Bomber Command to seek the cooperation of this organization, which was essential to the successful completion of the proposed mission.

On my way to Chengtu, on an army plane, I encountered an intelligence officer who was attached to the Twentieth. He was the man I would work with. When I explained my mission, he flatly declared that he would have nothing to do with SACO and would recommend that the Twentieth refuse to cooperate with any organization with which Tai Li was involved. It was necessary for me to spend a number of weeks overcoming this fundamental objection.

This young officer was exceptionally well informed concerning oriental affairs. He had traveled widely in Asia and knew more about what was going on in that part of the world than most American officers. He had served in SACO himself for months until he became convinced it would never be possible to prosecute the war successfully in cooperation with Tai Li.

The name Chengtu means the capital, or the Royal City. It was the capital of a kingdom centuries ago when China was fragmented between dynasties. Chengtu is situated in the fabulously rich Red Basin at the foot of the Tibetan tableland. When the weather is clear, which happens only a few times each year, one can look up from the streets of the city to the great snow peaks of the Chinese Himalayas.

Chengtu was traditionally old, rich, and conservative. It lies in the heart of one of the most densely populated areas of its size in the world. Its valley is about a hundred miles long and forty miles wide. It contained about six million people, equal in 1944 to the population of Belgium.

This large population was possible because, two thousand years ago, an engineering genius named Li P'ing designed a complicated irrigation system for the valley, supervised its construction, and left behind him specific instructions for its maintenance. The climate is mild and as a result of the plentiful water distributed by hundreds of miles of canals, the valley produces three crops each year. For centuries it has been a major center of Chinese civilization.

There was a substantial American and European population in Chengtu during World War II. This was largely centered around the fine West China Union University campus. There were British, Canadian, and American missions in Chengtu. Although they represented different churches in three countries, the missionaries were agreed that if the Chinese church were to become strong, it would have to have better leaders. They decided that Chengtu needed a Christian university. Individually, they were too weak to launch such an enterprise, but collectively it could be done. Plans were drawn up and presented to the mission boards in America, Canada, and Britain. These authorities would not approve of working with other denominations for the same cause, being grimly conscious of the heresies of their Christian brethren. The pious prelates at home refused to approve a united Christian effort to serve the church in China.

The missionaries in Chengtu were wiser than their superiors. They pooled their resources, bought adjoining plots of land, planned and built a university under the guise of establishing several small, independent denominational colleges. After this had been accomplished, the objection at home melted away and West China Union University was an acknowledged reality. It was one of thirteen Christian colleges and universities in China in which America had a paramount interest. These institutions did a great deal for China before the Communist conquest.

The new university found it hard to overcome the suspicions of such a conservative community as Chengtu. One of the greatest obstacles was the superstitious attitude of many people toward Western medicine. The Medical and Dental School became one of the most important parts of the university. Many rumors circulated in the city concerning the abuse of the bodies of dead babies and of other alleged barbaric practices in the big buildings on the new campus.

The confidence of the powerful landlord families and of the local warlords was won slowly by the demonstrated ability of the new medicines to cure disease. Once a grateful general asked how he could help an American doctor who had just cured a member of the warlord's family. The doctor had an inspiration. His class in anatomy needed cadavers. He explained that to be a doctor a man must be able to study human bodies. These were hard to get. Perhaps the general would be good enough to contribute the bodies of the soldiers who had been executed for breaches of military discipline. The general said he would provide all the bodies the hospital needed for instruction and research.

Thereafter, the hospital and Medical School regularly received a supply of fresh corpses from the barracks. This went on for some time, until the American doctor again met the general, who asked him if he was satisfied with the cooperation he was receiving. The missionary thanked the general and said that everything was fine except for one small matter. All the corpses the university had received from the barracks had been beheaded, which ruined the neck for teaching purposes.

The general beamed. "I understand your problem. Hereafter I will send them to you alive, and you can kill them any way you wish." The missionary was horrified, but found it hard to convince the general that such a procedure would not be desirable. Finally they compromised. The general was given a flask of chloroform with instructions for its use.

West China Union University was important from the standpoint of this book because it was typical of the great American and Western investment in money and human life in the cultural and educational institutions, and in the general welfare of the Chinese people. The influence of Christian schools, colleges, hospitals, and churches was great. Many of the leaders of Communist China were educated by American missionaries. If the political leadership in both China and the United States come to their senses, the foundation for future cooperation exists in the persons of Chinese and Americans who worked with each other many years in universities in China and America. If rapprochement is too long delayed, this unique foundation for cooperation will have vanished.

Much of the finest work in West China was done by Canadians. Two of them may serve as samples of the atmosphere of this remarkable institution, West China Union University. Gordon Agnew was a research dentist. He spent his vacations in the Tibetan highlands studying the relationship between decay of the teeth and diet. He discovered that the nomads on the grasslands, who ate mostly raw meat, had almost perfect teeth, while the people of the valleys, who had a varied diet more like our own, also had teeth like ours. Following this lead, he discovered the significance of vitamins in the control of caries, and thus made an important contribution to the welfare of people everywhere.

Frank Dickinson spent a lifetime in Szechwan, during which he helped to change the eating habits of millions of people. Once I traveled two days in a truck with him from Chungking to Chengtu, along with two fine roosters. These were the last of a flock which he had started with from Canada. All the others had died. One of the survivors was not too happy. Dickinson nursed him like a child all the way, but he died just after reaching his new home. The last surviving rooster, a fine White Leghorn, fathered a new generation of chickens in the Chengtu plain. Dickinson in the same way introduced improved strains of many crops ranging from the common grains to livestock. Szechwan had been a citrus center since the beginning of recorded history, but Dickinson improved local orchards by introducing choice strains from the West.

These men, and hundreds of men and women like them, helped to remake the face and the substance of China. They made Christianity what it always must be if it is to be worth its salt—a revolutionary force. Unfortunately there were too many conservative and racist Western missionaries in China. But many others were creative revolutionaries, very different from the God-bless-our-bondholders cult of many American churches. The ideals of the Christian revolutionaries undoubtedly contributed to the downfall of Chiang Kai-shek. Americans and Chinese may some day again cooperate in the service of those ideals.

I am reminded of a time when I was a small boy, and a frightened young student once rushed to our house to interview my father. He was the leader of a student group which called itself the Walden Club in our mission school. This club had incurred the wrath of the imperial viceroy by agitating against corruption in his administration. Thoreau's ideas were a strong force in the revolution against the Chinese imperial throne.

The boy said that the viceroy had invited him to go to the palace for an interview and had promised a safe conduct. But he had been warned by friends that assassins were planning to ambush him. The question he asked was, should he go? My father answered that if he was sure he would be in danger, he certainly should not go. But the boy objected. He said that he was a symbol, that if he showed fear at such a time, the progressive movement he represented would be shamed. He was desperately frightened, but he must go.

This high school student said something I can never forget: "Sometimes a man dares to die for what he believes." So he and my father prayed together, and the boy left our house to step into a sedan chair which the viceroy had sent to honor his young guest. A few blocks from our house, assassins cut him to pieces. But the progressive movement prospered exceedingly. In a few months, the Manchu emperor was overthrown.

The Chengtu plain was chosen as the forward base of the Twentieth Bomber Command for its attack on the industries of Western Japan. The altitude was low, the land was level, the climate better than in the Yangtze Valley. One of the great construction projects of World War II was the chain of airfields built here for the bombardment of Japan.

The land in the valley was very valuable. A single B-29 field required a runway nearly two miles long, ground for the approaches, the supply depots, the barracks, and everything else needed by a major military establishment. Around the bomber bases were grouped smaller fields for fighters to guard the valley from enemy attack. It was necessary to buy thousands of acres and to dispossess tens of thousands of men, women, and children—to drive them from their ancestral homes—in order to secure land for these bases.

American negotiators agreed on a price satisfactory to both parties and made every effort to protect the interests of the farmers who were losing their homes and farms. The American authorities then gave Chiang's representatives large sums of money—enough to pay the contract price to the people who were losing their land, their only source of livelihood. Much labor was needed to build the bases, so the dispossessed and thousands of additional men and women were employed in labor groups to work on the airfields and support enterprises.

Soon the Americans supervising the work discovered a new hostility toward them. Men, women, and children all worked together and they obviously did not like the Americans. A number of Americans were attacked; the situation became serious. Investigations proved that the farmers had not received the agreed price for their land. Large sums had stuck in various greedy hands on the way down to the farmers. The Americans were blamed; they had taken the land and failed to pay the full price for it.

The situation became so serious that an official of the American embassy in Chungking came to Chengtu with another large remittance and demanded that it be paid to the farmers. The Chinese army authorities stubbornly refused to permit the Americans to make the payments direct, so, again, the money was turned over to Chinese middlemen. After long recriminations, the landowners were paid an average of perhaps half the amount agreed upon in the original negotiations. And, of course, the Americans again were blamed. Tensions between Americans and Chinese rose sharply. By the end of the war, a year later, tension had become open hostility.

The common people on the plain were generally friendly. They were usually a sleek, well-fed generation and not unaware that the American air force was consuming large amounts of local farm produce, thus increasing farm incomes. Before the Twentieth actually moved in, the Chinese papers had announced that the American general would require an average of ten eggs a day for each of the ten thousand men in his command. Other supplies were ordered in proportion.

In the beginning, most of the shopkeepers, the middle classes in general, seemed to look on the Americans as allies, people to be treated as guests. There was a sincere effort to peg prices in Chengtu; they were written in Arabic numerals on almost all articles. There were cases of public exposure and punishment of merchants who had overcharged individual Americans. At the university there was a strong pro-American feeling, especially among the younger people. Because the Chinese staff had so little to live on, there was an official organization in the city which made generous allowances to families which entertained American officers and men at dinner to show them what Chinese home hospitality could be like. The governor, Chang Chun, was probably one of the better men in the Nationalist government. He and his wife seemed sincerely to wish to do what they could to maintain good relations with the American army.

But there were strong reactionary elements in the province which made it hard to maintain good relationships. There were articles in the papers recommending a virtual quarantine on the American forces. It was suggested that the foreigners living on the West China Union University campus should refrain from any contacts with the American troops. The mayor of the city offered as recreational facilities for the Americans two houses full of diseased prostitutes. These houses had to be declared off limits. The papers published articles urging decent women not to associate with the Americans. If a girl was seen talking to an American on the streets or in a restaurant, she could be arrested by the Secret Military Police and subjected to indignities. Slops were thrown from upstairs windows on Americans. Our vehicles were stoned in the streets. During this period, I cannot remember driving into the city at night without having stones thrown at me.

Everywhere there were the Secret Military Police, the Tai Li boys, watching what went on, keeping an eye on the Americans, listening to what they said, establishing barriers between them and the Chinese people. A strong, subtle anti-American propaganda was encouraged. Even by day, respectable Chinese women seen with responsible American men on the streets were surrounded by mobs that jeered and shouted, "prostitute, prostitute."

One day I was riding in a jeep on a road on top of a dyke above the plain. We speeded up to pass a bus. The driver of the bus speeded up, too, and, at just the right moment, turned his bus into the jeep to drive us off the road twenty feet down into the fields. This was deliberate. I was watching him and saw his sudden pull at the wheel of the bus, and watched his eyes as we escaped him. It was a small thing, an attempted murder of two American officers, but it was characteristic of the venomous undercurrent in Chengtu. I believe Tai Li knew what was happening and was at least partially responsible.

Because my dealings were with the Twentieth Bomber Command, I spent some time at the various airfields where this remarkable organization was active. It is difficult, a generation after our war, to describe what went on around Chengtu. Everything–gasoline, bombs, ammunition, and much of the food for American personnel–had to be flown over the Himalayas by long and dangerous routes. After thousands of Americans had been brought in and all the necessary ground establishments created, the great bombers themselves made their first landings. Each plane had to make two flights over the Hump loaded with gasoline before it could come in with bombs, reload the gas that had been left on previous flights, and take off for Japan.

One evening I counted more than seventy of the huge planes flying low over Chengtu. They moved slowly, ponderously, as they struggled for altitude. One was in obvious difficulty, wobbling uncertainly as it passed overhead; it dove into a mountain a few minutes' flight beyond us, and everyone in it was killed. This was the first bombing of Japan since the Doolittle raid. These planes were on the great-circle course for Kyushu.

Early the next morning I caught a jeep bound for Hsinchin, the Twentieth Bomber Command headquarters. Planes were already coming in from Japan, one after another. As far as I could see, they were all in good condition. At the field I saw the last planes land. I learned that every plane that had left this field had returned safely, with no casualties and only a few minor flak holes in wings and fuselage. A few planes from satellite fields had been lost, but, as a whole, the flight had been a great success and losses had been low.

The Twentieth was a highly efficient organization with many able men in key positions. Although these preliminary raids from the Chengtu bases fifteen hundred miles from the target area were nothing compared to the raids that were to hasten Japan's surrender a year later, they were of the greatest importance, both from the standpoint of the actual destruction of key Japanese industries and because of their propaganda value.

Such raids were possible only if the losses could be kept down. Losses continued to be low for several raids because security was so good the Japanese did not receive much advance warning of the actual target, although they seemed to know the planes were headed for Japan about as soon as they left the ground. Also, the superb defensive powers and the stamina of the planes and of the men who flew them kept losses at a minimum.

All this time Tai Li's Chinese Secret Military Police were complaining that they were not being treated with proper respect as allies because they were not being included in the briefings prior to each raid. At these briefings the target for the day was disclosed, together with the route to be followed by the bombers and other information of great potential value to the enemy. Finally, the American command relented and invited the Chinese intelligence officers in Tai Li's organization to attend a briefing.

This was before the first daylight raid by B-29s. By some evil coincidence, it was also the first time the enemy appeared to know all he should know for a successful defense. The American bombers were met miles from Japan above the Yellow Sea by a large flight of the latest Japanese fighters, and before the raid was over the Americans had suffered heavy losses. After that, the Tai Li officers did not attend briefings, and losses returned to normal.

During my visit to Chengtu, I was the guest of good American friends, William Fenn and his family. I had a legitimate excuse to be in Chengtu. The university hospital was the best in Free China and had turned over some of its facilities to the army. I needed an overhauling and had it in the hospital. Naturally, I did not tell my friends at the university that I was in SACO. I thought the matter a secret and have no idea how my connections could have become known.

I had helped to move the University of Nanking from its home campus to Chengtu in 1938, and many of my old friends invited me to dinner. I thought I noticed an occasional embarrassment on the part of my former Chinese friends in their contacts with me. They were friendly but seemed uncomfortable. After my departure, my host was delicately warned that it had not been wise for him to entertain a member of the Tai Li organization, even if he was an old friend formerly connected with the Christian colleges in China. Fenn's own usefulness had been somewhat impaired, he was told, by his friendship with a man known to be associated with the hated Tai Li.

My mission was at last accomplished, and I rode back by truck to Chungking. I never learned to enjoy air travel by army plane in China. There too many ways of getting into trouble when the terrain was so rough and wild and the emergency landing fields nonexistent for hundreds of miles. So this time I paid my way and rode on a Seventh Day Adventist Mission truck.

This was an experience that could have been enjoyed only in China a generation ago. It was an old, worn-out, ton-and-a-half Ford, literally falling apart. The carburetor was tied on with a piece of string. Every few miles it jolted off, the truck would stop, and the driver, a nice American named Floyd Johnson, would descend and tie it back on together with whatever other essential parts were in momentary danger of being lost. We were burning alcohol which gave us barely enough power to crawl up the steep hills.

On the truck was an overload of about a ton, and on top of a mountainous pile of luggage and whatnot rode twelve passengers, including five small American children. There was a young American missionary wife and her baby in the cab with Floyd. The passenger list also included a dog, several chickens, and two rabbits.

The weather was superb the first day, hot and utterly cloudless. We stopped in Chinese inns to eat, hung on in the blazing sunlight as branches sought to wipe us off the top of the truck, and had a fine time. The children were good sports. They had to be to survive in China.

We spent the night at a famous China Travel Service Inn at Neikiang. This is a fine old town, famous for candied fruits, friendly people, and bawdy inns. This new "hotel" was much more respectable than most, but still it was the sort of place that might have sheltered Chaucer's pilgrims. Nothing was private; the doors to the rooms were only chest high and the interiors fully exposed. The inhabitants did not bother to turn out their lights. Everyone liked everyone else and was friendly and courteous. We had a fine time.

The next day was not so pleasant. There were alternate heavy showers and glaring hot sky. The carburetor frequently fell off and we averaged a stop for repairs every twenty minutes all day long. Being a minister of the Gospel was somewhat of a hardship to Floyd, who could not express himself as freely as he wished. Finally I dropped off the truck on a mountain top above the Valley and got a coolie to carry my belongings down a precipitous stone path to our OSS headquarters in Death Valley.

Everything that needed to be done had been done in Chengtu. The foundation had been laid for an enterprise that might have worked considerable harm to the enemy. The project was approved by the Chinese Side as we called them, our Chinese counterparts in the Valley. It went to Tai Li for his final approval.

Weeks passed and nothing happened. We became more and more impatient and suspicious of Tai Li's intentions. Finally, General Hsieh must have urged our case too strongly. He was removed as our liaison and replaced by another major general less inclined to be friendly to the Americans. This new man knew no English and doing business with him was a major trial. Everything had to go through an interpreter, and after a matter had been explained in detail many times, our new Chinese liaison officer would shake his head and say the business was too complicated for a quick decision.

Before Derry Hsieh left us I had a talk with him. He told me that he wanted me to know he believed in our mission and had sincerely tried to help us to accomplish it. However, he said, there was a bottleneck which held up everything. Our project with the Twentieth Bomber Command, together with other important papers, was being held on General Tai Li's desk. They had been there a long time, and there they probably would remain.

Our West Point colonel, John Coughlin, commanding officer of OSS for China, Burma, and India, was visiting us. I told him the whole story, as I saw it, over a period of several days. I used the opportunity to brief the colonel on my contact through Mr. Chen with the secret societies.

I gave him all the information I had gathered which indicated that the Nationalist government and Chiang Kai-shek had lost the support of most of the Chinese people, and that Mao Tse-tung and his friends in Yenan were ready to take over at the appropriate time.

Finally he said: "Oliver, put it all down and I'll look at it." The next few days went into the preparation of a document which reported the plea of the three secret societies for American support for a moderate new government which would replace Chiang Kai-shek's regime as an alternative to probable Communist conquest of China after the end of the war. I supported my arguments by accounts of Tai Li's intransigence and hostility. I listed information I had secured from underground sources concerning anti-Americanism in Chiang Kai-shek's government and in his army. I listed evidence of trading with the enemy including approximate dollar values of the two-way commerce between Chiang's China and Japan; this information I had received secretly from the European who was director of the Maritime Customs Service in Chungking. I described many examples of the administrative corruption of Chiang's government. I made the strongest case I could for the abandonment of an American policy which supported Chiang Kai-shek and Tai Li. I recommended a new policy based on the need of the United States to win the war quickly. I urged that we support only those forces in China which supported our own objectives. I urged that we demand proof of such support before we threw hundreds of millions of dollars and hundreds of American lives into any rat hole.

This document was classified Top Secret. My description of its contents are based on my memory. I think it is important enough twenty-six years later to report that such a document was prepared, and later I will report what happened to it.

I showed the paper to the colonel. He read it carefully and said: "Oliver, I want to ask you only one thing. Are you sure of your facts?"

I said, "Yes, I am sure."

The colonel said: "This is so important that I will risk my career by sending it straight to Washington."

It was a long time before I learned what happened in Washington. The only reaction we discerned in the year ahead was the fact that neither Colonel Coughlin nor I was promoted; the colonel was replaced as commanding officer of the OSS in China, Burma, and India.

6 The Military Crisis

In the summer of 1944, a crisis developed in the cooperative Chinese-American war effort. American army commanders, under General Stilwell, were insisting with increasing vigor that the Chinese authorities live up to their obligations. Chiang's forces, including those under Tai Li, had almost ceased to fight the Japanese. Large amounts of war supplies, delivered to the Chinese forces by air over the Himalayas at great cost in American lives and American money, were either going into the black market or were being hoarded for use by the Nationalists in their coming civil war against the Communists. But when the war came four years later, hundreds of thousands of Nationalist soldiers joined the Communists. An American representative of the Rockefeller Foundation in Peking in 1949 reported that he watched a Communist victory parade in which Communist troops in American uniforms, bearing American arms, took three days to pass the reviewing stand. In the meantime, in 1944 the Americans, with the active and effective support of a relatively few patriotic Chinese, were doing almost all of the fighting in the China theater.

Commodore Miles still professed in 1944, and to the end of his life, that all was going well in China, and he continued to back Tai Li. The commodore was a good and honorable man but he was incapable of dealing with the sophisticated and slippery Tai Li. Miles put his theater commander, Stilwell, in an impossible position.

The navy contingent had expanded in odd directions. It had a camel corps in Chinese Turkestan, for what logical reason it would be hard to guess. It had outposts in outer Mongolia, why I cannot pretend to know, and no one in Death Valley ever gave a logical explanation. It had outposts all over the place, always secretive, always dominated by Tai Li, and not under the command of the man who was supposed to be the supreme American commander in China. In his book, Miles makes a good case for the work of the weather stations and other special groups scattered across China under his command.

But the navy groups often duplicated army, air force, or OSS groups. I can think of no logical reason for the navy contingent ever to have existed, other than for liaison purposes, on the Chinese mainland. During World War II in China, the American army and navy seemed to be fighting different wars. The waste in lives and material resulting from this duplication and rivalry should have been a scandal, but it was accepted by the involved Americans as part of our national tradition.

Here are some specific reasons for the growing strain between the Chinese and American armies.

Stilwell had been promised the full cooperation of the Chinese in the reconquest of North Burma. All he got were two divisions, which he trained and equipped in Assam until they were prize units. After a false start, these divisions began to push slowly from Assam toward China. As they got farther from their bases, the going got rougher, and they began to take heavy losses.

Under the Chinese-American military agreement, strong Chinese forces, trained and equipped by Americans, were supposed to cross the Salween and push from China toward India in a pincher movement. This would result in large Chinese forces being available to hit the rear of the Japanese; if this strategy had been followed, it might have saved many Chinese and American lives.

Y-Force was supposed to cross the Salween in March

1944. It did not cross for many months. Instead, there was silence on Salween. An American officer told me he was fined by his Chinese commander for firing at a Japanese across the Salween during this period.

Perhaps there was a deal between the Japanese and the Chinese commanders; this would have enabled the enemy to concentrate his strength against the American forces and Stilwell's two Chinese divisions. Whatever the reason, the result was months of bitter jungle warfare. The building of the Stilwell road was long delayed. The completion of the pipeline, essential for any large-scale American campaign in China, also was postponed and with it possible major ground operations against the Japanese in China.

Some observers guessed there were political reasons for the unwillingness to commit Y-Force to battle. In Yunnan province there were two Chinese armies. The governor, Lung Yen, was known as the last of the warlords. He had a large private army which was under his own command. His loyalty to the Generalissimo was open to question. It is my guess that Chiang Kai-shek was reluctant to endanger his own position in Yunnan by committing his best troops to a war against the Japanese. If this were the case, he should have told the Americans. Some of Stilwell's American officers believed the Chinese command wanted to create a situation which would discredit the American general and cause his recall. He was not popular on Chiang's staff. He was much too outspoken.

When the Chinese finally crossed the Salween, they sent only inferior troops who suffered heavy losses in their attacks on the Japanese garrisons at Tengchung and other towns. By this time, the Japanese in the strategic area in northern Burma had already been defeated without the help of Chiang's main armies.

The American aerial supply line across the Hump was a miracle. It cost America a great many airplanes and a large number of American lives to carry supplies by air into China before the opening of the road through Burma. These supplies made possible the operations of the Fourteenth Air Force and of the Twentieth Bomber Command. Also, by the summer of 1944, about nineteen divisions of the Nationalist army of the Chungking government had been equipped by airlift.

The Japanese were by now much concerned about the growing American and Chinese strength. It was apparent that they were going to try to capture the forward American bases, perhaps even Chungking and Kunming. They would then be free to concentrate their forces along the coast in anticipation of an American invasion (which the atomic bomb made unnecessary).

The Japanese drive, their last great offensive, had two prongs and lasted almost a year. The first prong struck across the Yellow River in northern Honan province. Its goal was the conquest of the Hanchung Valley, which would swallow several American bases and split Northwest China off from Szechwan. The Japanese then would have two options: to cross the mountains and go in either of two directions, toward Sian to the north, or toward Chengtu to the south, to capture the military and air bases near these cities.

The Chinese commander in this area was Tang En-po. His army was estimated at about three hundred thousand men. Tang was close to the Generalissimo, one of the old-style unregenerate generals. According to Americans who were in his area and saw what happened, he and his top colleagues had been making an enormous profit from trade with the enemy and did not want anything to disturb this pleasant situation.

Here a digression is in order. This trade with the enemy, also mentioned in the previous chapter, was quite open and caused constant friction between the Chinese and the Americans. According to American and European standards, trade with the enemy in wartime is considered treason. Chiang's government and his army were fostering this trade and derived a good part of their revenue from it.

When the Chinese moved into West China they were not able to take with them many of their factories in the East. They were cut off from the areas which produced most of their cotton, tobacco, silk, and wine, to mention only a few popular commodities. The Japanese and the Chinese who cooperated with their conquerors possessed much of China's productive power; it was to their joint advantage that they continue to sell these goods.

The Chungking government should have cut civilian consumption to a bare minimum and established small, essential, new industries in the west, together with such other new industries as might be required. Lu Chou-fu, an outstanding industrialist of my acquaintance, proved that this could be done. By my own observation, such facilities as did exist in Free China were not employed to capacity. Certain mills were closed down. Machine tools were for sale on the streets of Chungking because the owners could not compete with the cheaper, established industries of Japan and of the Chinese coastal cities.

Chiang chose to be dependent on East China, which of course gave aid and comfort to the enemy. The trade was entirely open. One of the main trade routes was the Yangtze River. Japanese control ended at Ichang, just below the gorges. An immense volume of goods was transported by small junks about fifteen miles from Ichang to a small town in Nationalist hands. Here there was an important station of the Chinese Maritime Customs, which openly collected a 5 percent ad valorum tax. The goods were transshipped to Chinese junks and Ming Sun steamers, and openly went up to Chungking.

I was invited by the European head of the Chinese Maritime Customs Service to take a long walk in the pine-clad hills across the Yangtze River from Chungking. He gave me figures for monthly and annual customs receipts derived from trade with Japan. They were fabulous. In addition to those who paid the nominal duty, there were countless merchants who followed the mountain trails and avoided customs payments. There were many routes by which Nationalist China exchanged goods with the enemy.

From Chungking to Sian, and in the little towns and large cities in between, one could buy an amazing assortment of Japanese goods, from bobby pins to alarm clocks, from dental equipment to motor cars. In the summer of 1944, I inquired on behalf of OSS concerning the possibility of buying a car. One of the Tai Li men assured me we could have one delivered, a new Japanese-assembled 1942 Buick, from Shanghai to Chungking for $3 million Chinese national currency, which at the time would have amounted to about $15,000 U.S. There were plenty of Japanese-made cars on the streets of the capital of China.

To pay for these goods, China had to drain her own resources. She sent out herbs, drugs, minerals, food supplies, many things she needed for her war effort. Also, she paid in her national currency, which was a contributing factor in the ungovernable inflation which helped eventually to destroy the Nationalist government.

A substantial proportion of American medical supplies sent over the Hump into West China was openly for sale in the black market in Chungking and other cities under Nationalist control. My informant in the Chinese Maritime Customs told me an important item in Chinese exports to Japan in 1943, '44, and '45 consisted of drugs given by the American people to Chiang's China. The rare new sulpha drugs were hard for many people in the United States to obtain, but I saw them freely displayed in the Chungking black market.

An evil result of this trading with the national enemy was psychological. Military and civilian leaders who had a stake in such a profitable enterprise were not anxious to disturb it. They could not support an aggressive attack by either Chinese or Americans on the Japanese and on lines of transportation to East China.

That was Tang En-po's situation when the Japanese began to mass for their drive in Honan. An aggressive commander might have forestalled the enemy by anticipating his attack. Guerrillas could have caused much damage behind the Japanese positions. But Tang and his officers were reluctant to disturb a pleasant and profitable situation. They hoped the Japanese felt the same way. But some of the Japanese were soldiers and realists.

When the Japanese finally moved forward, all bridges were intact, all roads open, and no one was ready to oppose them. A relatively small Japanese expeditionary force of perhaps sixty thousand men destroyed a "crack" Chinese army of three hundred thousand. It was a major disaster. The Chinese troops so misbehaved toward their own people that the peasants rose against them and are said to have disarmed about thirty thousand Chinese Nationalist soldiers. These peasants were not pro-Japanese or Communist. They were only interested in their own welfare. The arms they captured were used by guerrillas against the Japanese or were hoarded for the day when they would be needed for protection of the remote hill villages from other possible foes.

For a while things looked bad for the great American base at Chengtu. There was no army worthy of the name to stop the Japanese. But there were certain dangerous mountain passes through which the Japanese had to advance unprotected by their own air force, which had already been defeated by the Americans. The Fourteenth Air Force caught a strong Japanese mechanized task force in such a pass and practically destroyed it. The Japanese in this part of China never recovered.

There were other factors which contributed to the Japanese defeat. Some of their officers were inferior. Japanese supply lines were overextended. Finally, the Japanese command itself in this part of China was curiously lacking in initiative. Perhaps even the Samurai had been corrupted by their trade with Nationalist China. Tang En-po, who was such a colossal failure in Honan, was later one of the top Nationalist commanders in the Peiping area. Many Nationalist divisions in this area defected to the Communists during the civil war which followed World War II.

The other main Japanese strategic objective in 1944 was to close the gap between the Japanese in Hankow, on the Yangtze, and at Canton. This would isolate the Chinese in the coastal provinces from the rest of Free China and would destroy several dangerous American bases. This drive was mounted in Hankow and while it was being prepared, the Japanese base there was an ideal air target. The Fourteenth lost heavily in attacking Hankow, which was strongly guarded by Japanese fighters and antiaircraft guns.

One of the minor mysteries of World War II was why the Twentieth Bomber Command did not step in to help Chennault's men destroy the Hankow base. It was too big a job for the Fourteenth, but the Twentieth had several hundred planes available, ranging from B-29s to P-47s and P-51s. I was told that the Twentieth Bomber Command had a strategic mission, the bombing of the Japanese home islands, but if these planes had made a concerted attack with the Fourteenth on Hankow, it might have shortened the war. I had the impression that the commanders of the Twentieth did not much care what happened to Chennault.

In China, we knew that Chennault was not popular in Washington, and that he was in some ways an adventurer in the eyes of Stilwell and other professional military men; but his air force did one of the finest jobs done by any American military organization in the war. If things had gone only a little better for the Japanese, the Twentieth might have lost its China bases, partly as a result of its failure to cooperate with the Fourteenth in its attack on Hankow.

When the Japanese finally launched their drive

south, they made rapid progress in spite of determined efforts on the part of certain able Chinese generals to stop them, efforts magnificently reinforced by the Fourteenth. It was not fair for Americans in China to say, as many did, that the Chinese would not and could not fight. Given the incentive and the leadership, the Chinese are fine soldiers. If they have proper equipment, they are superb. MacArthur learned this fact the hard way in Korea.

The senior general in this area was Li Tsong-jen, who was the presidential choice of the people represented by my friend Mr. Chen. This was of course known in Chungking, and General Li could not be permitted to be victorious.

In spite of fine resistance at various points along the line of the Japanese advance, the Chinese were not able to stop them. Many American observers were present, and this is what they reported: The Chinese field commanders were hopelessly handicapped by the necessity of referring important decisions to Chungking. If the enemy was advancing, the local commander could not act on his own initiative. He would inform Chungking, and twenty-four to forty-eight hours later he would receive his orders. By that time it might be too late; his position might have been enveloped.

Under orders from Chungking, the Chinese in this campaign committed many tactical errors. Americans with them reported that time after time the Chinese drew their troops up in battle order across the valleys through which the Japanese were expected to advance. The Japanese thereupon advanced along the commanding ridges and flanked the Chinese positions.

The principal difficulty faced by the Chinese commanders in the Hunan area was diagnosed by some American observers as pure treason. These were some of the ablest men in China, and in the past successes of General Li Tsong-jen and the southwest group of generals had caused much discomfort to the minister of war, Ho Ying-ching, and others in Chungking. If they won a great victory this time, they would also win much prestige. This would have been embarrassing to Chiang and the Chungking government who had no desire to be replaced by popular, successful generals.

During the Japanese march south from Hankow to Canton, the Southwest generals controlled the armies in the center, while the Chungking clique controlled armies on both flanks. Several times when the Chinese were committed to battle, the Chungking armies on the flanks mysteriously withdrew, leaving the armies of the center to extricate themselves as best they could. They took heavy losses in the process and were weakened in relation to the Chungking forces.

Even so, the Japanese did not have an easy time. The Fourteenth imposed heavy losses on the invaders. In the end, the northern Japanese army merged with forces advancing from Canton, and the coastal provinces were cut off from the rest of China. The Americans lost Liuchow, Kweilin, and other valuable bases.

The Japanese eventually turned west toward Kweichow, Chungking, and Kunming. It looked for a while like they would succeed in destroying the main American bases, but the Stilwell divisions had finished their work in Burma and were flown across the mountains to stop the Japanese advance. They succeeded. It is interesting to speculate on what might have happened if the Chinese had cooperated in fulfilling the original X-Y-Z strategy. There might have been available at this time as many as sixty fully trained and equipped divisions to face the Japanese.

The defeats in Central China gave strong impetus to the plan to oust Chiang Kai-shek and his government and replace it with a more democratic regime. The southern generals combined with various progressive civilian elements, and a headquarters was set up in Kunming. The leaders of this clique began a long series of negotiations with other Chinese leaders, especially Lung Yen, the warlord of Yunnan, and with the United States authorities.

Through Mr. Chen and the secret societies, I had participated in this plot for some months. I believe the course of history could have been changed if Washington had supported the formation of a new moderate government in China.

The defeated armies, which believed they had been betrayed by the Chungking government, had withdrawn toward the sea, away from Chungking. Thus they were separated from the other Nationalist armies by a belt of Japanese forces. This had two effects. It insured a certain independence for these armies and their commanders, and at the same time Chungking was forced to rely on her own resources for salvation.

There were two governments in China for many years but we consistently recognized only one. When it became apparent to General Stilwell and to other clear-headed Americans in the Far East that the great American expectations of military aid from Chiang's government would never materialize, attention began to shift to the possibility of securing genuine cooperation from the Communist Yenan government in place of that which had been refused in Chungking. With much difficulty, consent was secured from Chungking for a small group of Americans to go to Yenan as "observers."

This group was under Colonel David Barrett. He was well qualified for such a mission. He had been a Chinese language student and had spent more than fifteen years in China. He spoke fluent Mandarin and possessed a rare ability to get along with the Chinese. He could quote Shakespeare and Confucius with equal facility. He was convivial, shrewd, and liked people. It was a pity that the prejudice in the American army against officers who were China specialists kept him from receiving any major commands.

The Barrett mission was few in numbers and limited in equipment but soon made itself at home in Yenan. One of the members was John Service, born in West China, a master of the language, who represented the State Department. Stelle, Domke, Whittlesey, and others all were marked by an exceptionally fine background in Chinese language, customs, and politics.

The Communists were anxious to make a good impression and, above all, to secure their share of the gravy in the form of American arms and equipment which was arriving in China over the Hump. They went all out to persuade the Americans that the Yenan government should share in the distribution of supplies. They made a good impression on most of the Barrett group.

While all this was going on, the American ambassador, Mr. Gauss, was replaced by General Hurley. First, General Hurley arrived in Chungking as a special envoy for President Roosevelt, a trouble-shooter whose mission it was to help straighten out the difficult situation in China. Hurley's first act in stepping off the plane was to emit an Indian warwhoop, which edified the diplomats who met him. Soon Gauss was on his way home and Hurley was a new broom that swept very clean. He was dined by Chungking notables and swallowed their propaganda hook, line, and sinker. What connection there was between him and Miles I do not know, but he was a partisan of the extreme conservative wing of the Kuomingtang, and Miles was on the same side of the fence.

There was a brief power fight between Stilwell and his adherents on one side and the Hurley-Miles clique on the other. It was a contest between well-informed and experienced men, some with many years of China experience, and conservative, poorly informed Red-haters.

The reports which came to headquarters from Yenan were full of enthusiasm for the possibility of successful cooperation between the United States army and the agrarian leaders of the Yenan government. Some of the best of these reports were written by Service. He was attached to Stilwell's staff as a political adviser. It was his duty to advise his commanding officer concerning the developments he saw in China. His reports were well written and were based on an excellent knowledge of political realities. These reports, and others like them, were used later by Senator Joseph McCarthy to wreck the diplomatic career of John Service.

The American army in China had one mission only and that was to defeat Japan. Everything else done by the army was supposed to be a means toward that end. Stilwell was determined not to commit the United States through his actions to any participation in civil conflicts

anywhere in Asia. At the same time, it was his obligation
not to overlook any possibilities for striking at Japan. It
was certainly not improper that his aide should send him
reports favoring the giving of supplies to the Yenan leaders for use in fighting the Japanese. Thousands of tons of
such supplies had been absorbed by the Chungking government and had quietly disappeared.

One reason some Americans favored giving Yenan a
chance to show what it could do was because there actually was a degree of democracy, as Americans understand
the term, to be found in the northwestern territories. Furthermore, morale in the Communist armies was reported
to be good compared to the Nationalist levies which were
usually half-starved and miserably led.

Morale among the Chungking troops was generally
bad for a multitude of reasons, many of which have already been mentioned. Soldiers and the lower grades of
officers were wretchedly cared for in every respect. The
men were conscripted, because under the *pao-chia* system
the rich were generally able to bribe the army to relin-
quish any claim on their sons. It was a common sight to
see conscripts trussed up with their hands tied behind
their backs, attached to a long rope, being led off to the
barracks.

When the men were wounded or sick their fate was
bad. All through the backcountry one could see disabled
troops hobbling home as best they could. They had been
given a few Chinese dollars (if they were lucky) and
turned loose. They would walk until the rags around their
feet were red with blood. They would beg from more for-
tunate travelers. Some who were stronger might become
bandits. Many died in the ditches and the dogs ate them.

Among the Old Hundred Names, as the common Chinese people often called themselves, to become a soldier was the worst fate that could overtake a man, equivalent to being sold into prostitution for a woman.

There were some good commanders who had good troops, but there were not many. Stilwell and his men had tried to reform the Nationalist army, which was a basic reason for the unwillingness of the top command in Chungking to entrust more of its divisions to the Americans.

The Yenan troops, according to the Americans who saw them, were another breed. They were even more poorly equipped than the Nationalists, but they were cheerful and well treated and apparently did not have to be hog-tied when they were conscripted. The Communists did a particularly good job of indoctrination so that the men appeared proud of the opportunity for service. The physical condition of the Communist troops impressed American observers as one of the greatest differences between them and those of the Chungking armies.

I have not gone into problems arising from Stilwell's personality. I supported him as well as I could while he was our commanding officer. But in later years books have appeared, especially Tuchman's *Stilwell and the American Experience in China, 1911–45,* which lead me to believe Stilwell was largely responsible for his own failure. Printed excerpts from his journal have convinced me that he did not really like the Chinese people.

The discontent of the Americans under Stilwell, with the treatment America had received from Chungking, the resentment of the reactionary elements in China against the Americans, and the misguided sympathies of

American conservatives for Chungking, sizzled and boiled to a head in the autumn of 1944.

It was obvious that Tai Li would not permit OSS to fulfill its mission in SACO. This fact was made particularly obvious to Colonel John Coughlin by the success which had been achieved by AGFTRS, a highly secret organization which consisted of OSS personnel attached to the Fourteenth Air Force and operating outside of SACO. AGFTRS was providing a major portion of the combat intelligence coming out of China, and proved what could be done under proper leadership when there was no immovable obstacle like Tai Li in the path.

We began to explore certain possible methods of circumventing the Tai Li agreement. At the time, we hoped that the Joint Chiefs of Staff might be persuaded that after two years trial SACO was a failure; OSS and the army could then try to find a new way to fight the Japanese. If Miles and the Navy contingent had not continued to support Tai Li it might have been possible to escape him.

OSS headquarters in Washington sent to China a certain Marine general as an inspector and goodwill emissary. He was a charming person and no doubt an excellent soldier, but he was not a diplomat. I was glad to see a high-ranking officer from Washington visit Tai Li. OSS had been handicapped in China by the low rank of its key personnel. The general might have accomplished considerable good if he had been better prepared, or possibly if he had been better informed concerning what to expect.

Tai Li gave him a fine banquet in which there was much drinking and making of toasts. The American general became noisier as the liquor began to work. His junior officers looked on in horror. Tai Li sat like a hawk, skillfully egging his victim on to make ever franker statements about SACO, about the Generalissimo and the Madame, about China.

The younger American officers tried to silence the general but Tai Li lashed out with an order to leave the general alone and let him have his say. And after he had said it, Tai Li was in a fury. The smoldering antagonisms in SACO were brought out into the open, together with a good many secrets that might better have been left untold. Among other things, the American general made very uncomplimentary remarks about Madame Chiang. This indiscretion created a dangerous diplomatic incident which hastened the recall of Stilwell and came close to rupturing Sino-American relations. It was one of the critical moments of the war in the Far East.

The general was placed under arrest and sent back to Washington. I do not know what was his punishment. This almost unknown but serious incident shows highlights of the basic weaknesses of American policy in Asia in our times. Delicate negotiations are too often turned over to a friend of a friend of someone in high places, and the result is that American prestige is tarnished. There is no substitute for knowledge and wisdom in human relationships. The Case of the Drunken General greatly weakened the American position in China. For a time, Tai Li insisted that OSS be barred from future operations in China.

The final showdown came when Stilwell bluntly demanded that the Chinese conservative clique in Chungking live up to its commitments. He demanded that he be given command responsibility over Chinese troops in place of his empty title as Chief of Staff to Chiang Kai-shek. He demanded that certain reforms be made in the Chinese army itself to make of it an effective fighting organization. Chiang Kai-shek complained to President Roosevelt, and Hurley backed Chiang. In the background was Miles; he continued to support Tai Li and all that Tai Li stood for.

So General Stilwell was recalled. When he left he took with him a goodly portion of the intelligence and the drive which had distinguished the American military effort in the Far East. He left behind him some good men. There are those who speak well of Wedemeyer who replaced him, but Stilwell was a man and a soldier in the grand tradition in spite of his human faults.

Stilwell's defeat was a defeat for both China and America. It was followed, in December 1944, by a carefully organized slaughter of the intellectuals, artists, writers, and others who were members of the group which was working to replace the Chungking government with a new moderate regime friendly to the United States. Homes were invaded by soldiers who shot fathers of families and left their bodies in the streets to warn others not to think dangerous thoughts. Some of my friends who witnessed it called it a massacre. Most Americans, including those in high places, either did not care or never knew what happened.

By this time I was completely committed, intellectually and emotionally, to the need to oust Chiang and his clique from power. The history of mankind might have taken another direction had Li Tsong-jen and his group, supported by the three great secret societies, received American encouragement to create a new moderate, popular government in Free China. Mao Tse-tung might not now be in Peking, and American troops might never have fought in Korea and Southeast Asia.

With each passing year, American mistakes in China in 1943 through 1945 loom larger and more ominous in their consequences.

7 Aftermath

The replacement of Stilwell by Wedemeyer marked a turning point in the history of American relations with China. Regardless of Wedemeyer's excellent personal qualities, as compared to the acidity of Vinegar Joe, I believe American policies in Asia started downhill at this time. We won the war with Japan, but we lost China. If we had not lost China, we might not have fought two unnecessary wars in Korea and Vietnam.

The policy of blind support for the Kuomingtang, which began with the ouster of Stilwell, was a break with our traditional policies in China. In backing a single Chinese faction with arms, supplies, and men, we abandoned our traditional Open Door policy. We did just what Hay's policy was intended to prevent others from doing.

An immediate result, as far as OSS was concerned, was the placing of our relations with the Chinese in the hands of the smoothies of the Kandy set, in that city where Wedemeyer had served in Ceylon prior to his transfer to China. While some of the Kandy Kids, as they were lovingly known, were among the best people in OSS, others had to be seen to be believed. I remember several of them as military and naval hippies twenty years ahead of the Hippy era.

After the Case of the Drunken General, Tai Li treated OSS with a very high hand. There were rumors that the organization would be forced to abandon China entirely. This would have been a blow to our military forces which relied on OSS for combat intelligence. General Wedemeyer was able to secure for OSS another chance.

During this time, when the war news did not look good for the Allies, when the armies of Eisenhower were stalled along the West Wall, and particularly during the Battle of the Bulge, when for a time it looked as if the Germans might reverse the tide of the war, the Tai Li organization and the conservative Chinese oligarchy he represented were sometimes openly hostile not only to OSS but to the U.S. Army.

This was particularly apparent in India where there was a kind of secret war between the OSS and Tai Li's agents. Chinese military intelligence, under Tai Li, was miffed at the reluctance of the Twentieth Bomber Command to take them into its confidence. In Calcutta there was an American colonel who was A2 (intelligence chief) for the Twentieth Bomber Command. Obviously, he was a repository for information concerning the activities, present and future, of that highly successful organization. This story concerning him, as far as I know, was never reported in America.

One evening this colonel was kidnapped. A big car slipped alongside him and a man jumped out to force him into it at pistol point. A blindfold was placed over his eyes and the car raced for some unknown destination. He had an opportunity to see something of his assailants and was particularly struck by the cultured Oxford accent of one of his captors. It was a voice and accent he knew well: it belonged to a Chinese major attached to the Tai Li group in Calcutta. The colonel tried to find out what they wanted of him. He did not learn anything concrete, but got an impression that he was being spirited away to a safe place where he would be persuaded to tell the Chinese what he knew about the war plans of the Americans.

It was obvious that when they had learned what

they wished from him, they would have to kill him. Death after torture did not appeal to the colonel, so he determined to make a break. He was aided by the fact that the blindfold had not been securely tied. By tilting his head and looking down, he could see a little of what was going on. He noticed the position of the lever on the car door and saw a red light in front of the car. His hands had been tied behind his back, but at the right moment he threw his shoulder against the lever. The door opened, and he was in the street. The major lunged out after him and might have captured the American if he had not turned his ankle. The colonel got away, and the Chinese went about their business, whatever it was.

There were other similar incidents in Calcutta. An OSS sergeant was charged by a Chinese holding a knife; the sergeant shot him dead. One evening an OSS major saw a hand with a knife descending on him as he came around a corner. He grabbed the arm and in the ensuing struggle was slightly cut. The Chinese got away.

One of the strangest aspects of Sino-American relations during this period was the vicious persecution of Americans in the United States who believed that the Nationalist Chinese were not fully supporting the American war effort and had the temerity to say so. First, there was the Case of the Six Suspects.

In June 1945, there was a big spy scare involving three men connected with the State Department and three professional writers. The government employees were accused of the theft of secret documents, which had been turned over, it was charged, to the writers. Two of the people involved, Philip J. Jaffe and Emanuel S. Larsen, were fined as they apparently had been to some degree technically guilty. The charges against three of the others were refused by a federal grand jury on the grounds that there was no evidence. The last defendant had to wait for several months until the case against him was nolle prossed.

The case of John Service has been in the news off and on for nearly thirty years. He started a career in the State Department as one of the few men in the Foreign Service genuinely qualified as China experts. He was born in Chengtu of missionary parents and spoke the language extremely well. As a political adviser to General Stilwell, he made reports to the General. These reports Ambassador Hurley, and others like him, did not approve. These reports have haunted him for most of his life.

After Hurley's policies of placating the Nationalists failed and he returned to Washington, he made furious charges against Service and George Atcheson, another able China career specialist. There was a Senate investigation which revealed no treason. The secretary of state pointed out that Service's only offense apparently lay in the reports he had presented to General Stilwell and that in making these reports he had not been insubordinate, as was charged by Hurley, but had merely been fulfilling his duty. Service was responsible to Stilwell and not to Hurley. The case collapsed. Years later, Service was denounced again by Senator McCarthy during the witch hunts led by the senator in 1954–55.

John Davies is one of the ablest men I have met in our Foreign Service. He was also a political adviser to Stilwell, stationed in New Delhi, the rear echelon headquarters of the China-Burma-India theater. Davies was born and brought up in China and was expert in the language. He had served with exceptional intelligence and courage through the worst days of the war in the Far East. He had the respect of the military because of his good sense and courage. Once when he was flying the Hump, he had to parachute into the jungle. He led the survivors of his plane through rough jungle country for several weeks until they finally reached civilization.

Davies's offense was in doing his duty too well, in being intelligent and outspoken. So when Hurley took over in China, Davies had to be punished. He was removed from his post. At first, according to the story I heard at the time in Delhi, he was demoted to vice-counsel at Basra, one of the worst posts in the Foreign Service, and a place where his knowledge of China could inconvenience nobody. Then the sentence was transmuted: he was sent to Moscow.

Years later, he was on duty in Germany when Senator McCarthy ran amok. Davies eventually was forced to resign and went into exile in Lima, Peru, where he sold furniture for a living. He was cleared many times by the FBI, but remained officially unemployable. He was finally rehabilitated by the Nixon administration.

I went to the Shanghai American School with both Davies and Service. I was in the army while they were in the diplomatic service in 1944 and '45. These are two brave, patriotic men who have been treated abominably by their country. Pro-Chiang Kai-shek forces have relentlessly persecuted them.

My brother, John Caldwell, was head of the China branch of the Office of War Information. John was invited to address the naval military government school at Columbia University sometime in 1944. He used this opportunity to describe the activities of the Miles naval group in China. Not long thereafter the FBI descended on him and he had a very unpleasant time. Five times the FBI "grilled" him; this upset his wife who was seriously ill. There was no case against him that even the wildest wartime hysteria could discover. He was left alone after suffering inconvenience and hardship.

There is a dangerous pattern in the systematic persecution of China experts who have been brave enough to criticize our China policies. It looks very much like the Soviet strategy of dealing with people whose opinions are unorthodox. Of course, we don't shoot our China dissenters, or put them in concentration camps. We just ostracize them, slander them, and take away their livelihood.

Persecution merely because some vengeful persons in or out of authority do not approve of one's views concerning China, honestly expressed and in proper channels, is intolerable. It has been a fact of American life for a generation. It is still a serious issue in the 1970s. It is a question of whether America wants trained, honest, competent people to shape American policies in the Far East, and whether there can be an open and honest debate concerning every aspect of our Far Eastern policy. It is particularly strange that it has been so dangerous for an American to tell the truth as he sees it about Nationalist China.

America sowed the wind in China during the Hurley-Miles period in World War II and later during the Joseph McCarthy era. For a quarter of a century, our China policy has been dominated by people who know very little about China or Asia.

8 Making War in India

In the fall of 1944, Colonel Coughlin ordered me to report to rear echelon headquarters in New Delhi for special assignment. I was to be acting director of Morale Operations (MO), until further notice, and was again involved, as I had been in Death Valley, with the creation of black propaganda—the kind that did not pretend to tell the truth.

New Delhi seemed like heaven after Death Valley. I was assigned to a comfortable barracks. I had a private room and my personal servant. We had a formal dining room where we were waited on by turbaned Indian waiters. We lived in the manner to which British Colonial military officers had become accustomed.

I reported to the headquarters of OSS on Ferozshah Road and immediately fell into a den of young lionesses. The Morale Operations staff consisted, as I remember, of seven young American women. Most of them seemed to hate each other, but united in common opposition when I appeared to take over.

In New Delhi I encountered the true OSS for the first time. It was a unique military organization which enlisted civilians, men and women, and all ranks in the army, navy and marines for unconventional undercover, and frequently hazardous, duty. It appeared that much of the work was done at cocktail parties. Command responsibility was supposed to be given to the most competent person available for a particular job without regard to rank or other mundane considerations. Theoretically, a civilian girl or an army sergeant could command a detachment which included colonels.

My seven lionesses were nice girls, individually. Three of them were brilliant. None of them had had any experience in psychological warfare and therefore should never have been assigned to MO in India or anywhere else. Three of them of equal rank had been taking turns fighting each other for the responsibility of heading the unit. Under them, in widely scattered outposts in China, Burma, and India, were a number of other small units, three of which were commanded by elderly majors who got tired of the treatment they were getting from the girls and demanded that a male officer take over.

Unfortunately, the colonel appointed me without prior approval from MO headquarters in Washington, which quickly repudiated me. The majors also resented having to work under the direction of a captain. So, for six months, I worked for my colonel, frequently blocked and bypassed both by Washington and the girls and the majors on my staff. It was not a dull assignment.

If I were making arrangements for an ideal war, I would insist that no women be permitted in any forward areas. Regardless of the gallantry and dedication of individual women, the injection of sex into a wartime situation establishes an intolerable obstacle to discipline without which not much of anything can be achieved.

Our headquarters were in a villa which OSS had rented from an American dentist for the duration of the war. He had lived very well indeed, and with the villa we had inherited one of the best chefs in New Delhi and a staff of servants. Each male officer attached to the villa had to take his turn as duty officer for a weekend. This meant that I had complete control of the villa, the cook, and the servants one Saturday and Sunday out of every six. I would generally invite members of my staff and friends from other units to a formal dinner on Saturday night. Sometimes, I would shoot one or two wild peacocks for the occasion. An adult peacock would weigh about eighteen pounds, much of it white meat.

According to the Pentagon, those of us who lived in New Delhi were living under jungle conditions. Therefore we were permitted to purchase tax free each month a jungle ration consisting of a liberal allowance of Scotch, bourbon, and gin. Additional liquid refreshments were always available because a few miles away there was a British distillery which manufactured excellent gin.

This was a new experience for a boy who had been brought up in a Methodist missionary's home. I was not a teetotaler, but I was appalled by the amount of liquor which we consumed. At ten o'clock each morning, the waiter would appear to offer us a choice of tea or gimlets made of local gin and limes. I had the impression that a number of people in our headquarters were alcoholics and I have often wondered what happened to them.

I had already decided what was to become more apparent as my military career continued: I was probably, in many ways, one of the most inept soldiers in the U.S. Army in World War II. In China, I was a maverick generally regarded with suspicion by conventional soldiers, both American and Chinese. I had alienated my former Chinese civilian friends by my association with Tai Li whom I despised. I certainly did not fit in well with my young lionesses, their friends, and the savage intriques in the headquarters of a large wartime army. I decided to do my best to help the colonel by bringing order out of the glorified cat fight which I had inherited from him. I hope we did do a few worthwhile things while I was in charge.

One of our first projects involved printing several million Japanese railroad tickets. These were tickets from Tokyo out into the country to various cities on various rail lines. Other tickets entitled the bearer to depart from Kobe, Osaka, and other Japanese cities for cities and towns in remote parts of Japan. These tickets were supposed to be dropped by our bombers over Japanese cities and it was expected that millions of such tickets, undistinguishable from those bought at the railroad station, could help to paralyze the Japanese rail system. We hoped that millions of people would be traveling all over Japan, by courtesy of OSS, to the consternation and confusion of the Imperial Japanese government.

I received conflicting accounts regarding the success of this plan. I still think it was as sensible as an OSS idea someone else dreamed up which led to the release of thousands of bats from American airplanes over Japan, each bat carrying a small firebomb set to go off hopefully after the bat found a new home under the eaves of a Japanese house. The bats were expected to set great fires in Japanese cities. For reasons I never learned, the bats were not successful arsonists.

I was really proud of our masterpiece in black psychological warfare. This grew out of prolonged bull sessions of our staff which now included a young male naval officer. We decided to try to cripple the Japanese army in Burma, which was much larger in number than the small Allied forces facing them, by destroying the confidence of the enlisted men and junior officers in their senior officers. So we drafted a Japanese army general order which went something like this: "His Imperial Majesty orders that all field grade officers [majors and above] and general officers guard their lives at all times. His Majesty requires that in the event of combat, such officers retreat to a safe position in order that their lives may be preserved for the greater glory of the Empire."

Three Japanese officers were prisoners of the British in the Red Fort, which is a tremendous, fortified mogul palace in Old Delhi. Since I was responsible for the development of this particular project, I spent considerable time with British officers securing the cooperation of these Japanese officers in the duplicating of a Japanese general order. Our intelligence brought us a batch of the Japanese paper on which such orders are printed. One of our prisoners wrote the order in the correct form and language. It was modeled after a captured general order. After our draft had been carefully scrutinized by some of our Japanese-language experts to make sure that we were not being deceived by the prisoners, several of these orders, properly classified according to standard Japanese army practice, were printed. The next step was to dirty them by dropping them on the ground, walking on them, and folding them so that they would appear to have fallen out of some senior officer's pocket.

A few weeks later, one of our agents distributed a number of these false orders on jungle trails which he had reason to believe were used by Japanese patrols. We were told that it was not a coincidence that shortly thereafter when our guerrilla forces ambushed several Japanese units, the enemy did not stand to fight but retreated in disorder.

There have been many cities built at the site of Delhi during the past two thousand years. I loved the

Indian countryside and have warm memories of long rides and walks in the area round New Delhi. The plains around the city supported many thousands of antelope and millions of game birds, ranging from quail to wild peacock. We supplemented our diet by shooting game for the kitchen. Beef was hard to get in India and the troops needed fresh meat.

Most of the farmers around New Delhi were Hindus and as such they could not kill any living thing. Herds of antelope sometimes would descend on a man's farm and reduce the family to starvation by eating the crops. There were also thousands of monkeys in that area, some of which were vicious and attacked people who were forbidden by their religion to defend themselves. The farmers were generally happy to help us find game; sometimes our men would shoot a monkey which had attacked their children.

But it was dangerous to harm the peacock, which is sacred to the Goddess Parvati. One could get himself lynched if he were seen shooting a peacock. In retrospect, I am ashamed of the technique I developed to get around this problem. During the mild Indian winter, I drove on a moonlight night along an Indian road and silhouetted the trees against the moon. I would pick out a large bird and shoot it. I found there was a fifty-fifty chance that it would be a peacock. Otherwise it would be a buzzard. Thus we kept ourselves well supplied with peacocks. At that time my conscience bothered me not at all, since peacocks were among the worst enemies of the farmers.

There are low hills not far from New Delhi and considerable wild land. Sometimes we would build a bonfire after dusk while we roasted antelope steaks. This aspect of my life in New Delhi helps to counteract dark memories of some of my official activities while in India.

During the winter of 1944–45, our headquarters in New Delhi experienced a number of breaches of security in dealing with Chinese officials. Since Chiang Kai-shek was our full-fledged ally, Chinese officers in India sometimes demanded information concerning American plans. When such information was shared with them, sometimes the Japanese received the news; this happened too often for coincidence. I was called in by the head of the OSS Security Office and asked if I would undertake a counterespionage assignment to find out who in the Chinese military was betraying us. I was selected because of my knowledge of Chinese. I selected two of our girls to help me. Joy was tall, fair, handsome, and about twenty-seven; Rosemary was short, dark, vivacious, pretty, and about twenty-four. Both spoke excellent Mandarin.

I went to Calcutta for a briefing on what was going on in our relations with the Chinese in that city. I found an undeclared war between the OSS men and women in that city and the members of Tai Li's military intelligence group. I learned that two young Chinese sisters, both of them refugees from Malaya, were suspected of being double agents of the Chinese Secret Military Police and of the Japanese army. The girls arrived in Calcutta after the fall of Singapore. They said their parents had sent them out to carry on the national war against Japan. Sympathetic Americans sent them both to mission schools.

By early 1945, the older girl was married to a respected businessman. However, our agents had followed her around for several weeks and had a list of purchases which she had made of electrical components. This list constituted most of the parts for a small radio sending set. The younger girl, beautiful and nineteen, had left school and led a full social life. She had dated several Americans in our OSS headquarters. She showed a preference for men connected with communications. We then had no proof she was an enemy agent.

Shortly after I returned to New Delhi, I was called to the security officer and told that two things had happened. The girl had been given, by one of her dates, what appeared to be valuable military information in Calcutta. She was seen to go immediately to her sister's home and our intelligence people were convinced that the information had been sent immediately to the Japanese on her sister's radio. There was enough supporting information to require that she be eliminated. I hope our information was not wrong. The number of people in this century who have suffered because they were supposed to be spies, whether they were or not, must be large.

My second piece of information was that the girl had been making frequent visits to New Delhi and had become engaged to a young American major. He was a nice, open-faced, innocent, young man. He had invited Joy, Rosemary, and me to a party where he was to announce his engagement. I was given the job of telling the major that he must go through with the party but that his fiancée would be immediately arrested after the party and treated the way spies are treated.

I cannot forget my conversation with this heartbroken and bewildered young man. At first he refused to believe that the girl was a spy. Then he refused to hold the party. I told him that he was under orders to go through with the charade. It was important that the party be held because it would give Joy, Rosemary, and me a chance to see if she had any special relationship to any of the Chinese officers in the Chinese embassy who also had been invited to the party. Our New Delhi security people believed she had a partner in the embassy to whom she gave information she secured from the Americans, which her partner then radioed to Japanese headquarters in Burma.

The girls and I were miserable. A number of other Americans present knew what was happening, and the result was very heavy drinking as people tried to forget what was about to happen to a beautiful, young woman who was suspected of being a spy.

A Chinese major general from the embassy, a Tai Li man, was one of our suspects. He led the girl to a sofa in front of a fireplace and they sat there talking. I sidled over and sat on the other end of the sofa and leaned back, pretending that I was taking a nap. All I heard was a long lecture from the elderly general on the evils of sexual frustration, and finally a proposition to the girl. Thereupon she started to laugh and leaned over and kissed me on the cheek, then left both the general and me on the sofa. I assumed that she was telling me she knew I was a plant, an American intelligence agent. Shortly after this, the party broke up and the girl disappeared.

After this summary disappearance of a beautiful girl who probably was a spy, Joy, Rosemary, and I experienced a chill in our relations with the Chinese embassy. We were convinced that the Chinese authorities knew what had happened and also knew about our assignment. Both of the girls told me they were nervous and wanted to carry pistols in their handbags. I went to our security officer who refused to issue guns to the girls. He said there was obviously no possible danger to either of them. I tried unsuccessfully to get him to change his mind because all of my instincts told me that the Chinese would retaliate. I slept with my door locked and a .45 under my pillow. By day, I carried a .32 in a shoulder holster under my jacket; this was contrary to military regulations which forbade us to carry arms in New Delhi. I felt the girls were entitled to equal protection.

A few days later, Joy told me that she and Rosemary had been playing tennis at the Chinese embassy that afternoon and that the senior military attaché told her in plain words that they knew exactly what the three of us were trying to do. Joy told me that she was very frightened. Fear was not a characteristic of this girl. She was a diabetic who, in some way I never discovered and she was unwilling to explain, had succeeded in passing the strict OSS physical examination. She was a tall, strong, athletic girl who had spent a good deal of time in China and spoke Chinese well.

The next Saturday night I locked myself in my room and went to bed with my pistol handy. About eleven o'clock I was awakened by what I thought was a puppy crying at my door. I became fully awake when I heard a faint voice say, "It's Joy. I am hurt." When I opened the door, I saw a badly injured girl with blood all over her. She had received a bad blow on the back of her head; there were cuts on her face; and both hands and arms were badly cut. Before she went into a coma, she told me that after dinner she decided she would go to our office on Ferozshah Road to get her personal address book. She wanted to write letters on Sunday. There was a full moon and New Delhi was considered a safe city.

Before she had gone far from her quarters on the curved road which led up to the main thoroughfare where our headquarters were located, she heard a car coming around the bend back of her. When she turned to look at the car, it was about forty feet behind her and the headlights had been turned off. She said she heard the motor roar and she jumped toward the center of the road to escape being run over. The car had right-hand drive, and in the left seat there was a man who swung a blackjack at her, catching her in the back of the head and knocking her to the road, half conscious, on her face. The car then stopped and the driver started to back up to roll over her. Joy managed to tumble into the deep ditch beside the road which was full of broken bottles. She landed on the glass and was badly cut. She picked up a piece of glass as her only weapon and saw a man get out of the car with a pistol in his hands and come toward her. At that juncture, the headlights of another car appeared around the bend. The man hastily jumped into his car which drove away. Joy told me the car was a blue Zephyr sedan belonging to the Chinese military mission and that the man who came out with the pistol was a military attaché we both knew well. He was a Tai Li man.

I made Joy as comfortable as I could, and, full of rage, I called our American field hospital. The sergeant I talked to didn't believe me when I said that one of our girls had been seriously hurt. He said that I was drunk. It took several calls and a threat of court martial to persuade the gentleman to send an ambulance.

Joy never fully recovered from her wounds. She drifted in and out of a coma and was unable to talk coherently for many weeks. When I reported what she had told me to the OSS security officer, he laughed in my face. He said it was impossible that her injuries could have been the result of an attack by anyone. After all, everyone knew Delhi was a perfectly safe place. He reminded me that she had diabetes and said that she had undoubtedly passed into a coma naturally and then fallen into a ditch. He did not explain how she came out of the coma under such circumstances and then managed to walk two miles, leaving a trail of blood all the way to my quarters. This man was by profession an automobile salesman but was omniscient in both military and medical affairs.

Joy remained in the field hospital for many weeks and eventually was flown home to New York where she joined her husband. He had been serving in Europe while she was in India. After a long stay in the base hospital, the army sent her home with a bill for two thousand dollars. The OSS refused to compensate her because this major refused to admit that he had made a mistake. Finally, another OSS officer, Philip Crowe, who had been a special friend of both the two girls and myself, went to a senator and told him the story. In a few days, OSS sent a two-thousand-dollar check to Joy's husband.

A year later, in Washington, when I was in the State Department, I received a telephone call from a young woman in New York who said: "You don't know me, but we have a mutual friend. Joy asked me to call you to say good-bye for her because she is dying." A few days later I saw her obituary in the *New York Times*.

9 The Great Earth

In 1944 the Air Transport Command carried 231,000 tons of supplies over the Hump. In the last month before the Japanese surrendered, American planes carried into China about 74,000 tons of food, arms, munitions— everything needed in modern war. This victory in logistics, the science of supply, was a phenomenal accomplishment. Yet when the goods had reached Kunming, or one of the other China bases where Hump planes landed, the journey was far from ended. Most of the supplies that went into China had to be distributed to remote Chinese or American bases, some of them more than a thousand miles from Kunming.

There was an organization called Combat Cargo which flew unarmed cargo ships in the combat zones where ATC was not permitted to go. They were heroes still unsung. To fly with them as a passenger also sometimes required a certain amount of heroism, for these pilots were exceedingly casual about flying over terrain where there were no landing fields, in uncertain weather, where an occasional enemy fighter might be lurking. But sometimes there were no airfields available or not enough planes to meet the need. Then it was necessary to move supplies by land, and that provided adventure enough for anyone.

Traditionally the rivers of China furnished the best and quickest avenues for transportation and goods could go overland between rivers only on the backs of men or animals. Between 1927 and 1937, Chiang built thousands of miles of crude motor roads reaching through some of the most beautiful country on earth. Traveling on these highways was very difficult. The distances resemble those in America, and in the lonely mountain country there were bandits. During World War II there were very few service stations in West China. We had to carry our spare parts and be able to make our own repairs, and we generally carried enough gas for a round trip. Chinese busses and trucks, for the most part, ran on alcohol or used charcoal generators to make carbon monoxide.

Our United States forces operated various convoy routes against powerful odds. At first the bandits had a fine time, for American troops were ordered not to fire on Chinese under any circumstances. In some areas Americans were ordered to carry no firearms. This caused a great deal of bitterness among American victims and certainly did not deter the bandits.

This problem came to a head when a large convoy started for southern Yunnan under the command of an American major. When the vehicles reached a pass in the mountains, they were fired on by men in Chinese army uniforms. The Americans surrendered to the "bandits," who stripped their vehicles, then stripped the men themselves to their underclothes. The American flag was torn down, ripped to bits, and the pieces stamped on by the marauders. Then the Americans were all forced to kowtow to the bandit chief, which means to get down on the hands and knees and bump the head on the ground.

When the men got back to Kunming, feeling ran high among the Americans. The next convoy was a smaller group headed by a lieutenant. He had a conference with his men and they swore to fight to the end if they were attacked regardless of orders. When they reached the danger zone, they were attacked by what appeared to be the same gang. The Americans dove for

Inner Mongolia

SHANSI

Loess Cave

SHENSI

Yellow River

KANSU

Yellow River

HONAN

Sian

TSING Paochi LING MTS.
Miaotaisze
Hanchung

HUPEI

TSINGHAI

Nanchung

SZECHWAN

River

HUNAN

Mienyang

Chungking

Chengtu
Camp Oasis

Luhsien

Tsunyi

Ipin

KWEICHOW

Pichieh

Weining Weining Lake

Yangtze

Suanwei

Chanyi

YUNAN

KWANGSI

Kunming Kunming Lake

Convoy route
Route for Paul Fanning rendezvous
☐ SACO headquarters
■ U.S. Navy Camel Corps

C.C. Weiss
S.I.U. Cartographic Laboratory
Source used for spelling of Chinese place names is
Hammond World Atlas (Maplewood, N.J.: Hammond, Inc., 1967).

the ditches with their tommy guns and, in a short time, killed several of the bandits without themselves suffering any losses.

The lieutenant expected to be court-martialed but he wasn't. He became an unofficial hero. The general order against firing on bandits was rescinded and thereafter there were some sharp brushes with outlaws. Gradually, the bandits, who frequently were mutinous soldiers and sometimes were merely half-starved peasants, began to fear American soldiers, and attacks became less frequent. Sometimes the attackers appeared to be regular Nationalist troops. Up to the end of the war, traveling in many parts of Free China could not be recommended as a pleasure tour.

In March 1945, I was relieved, at my own request, of my assignment in New Delhi. I received a new assignment in intelligence on the staff of my friend Major Gustave Krause. It was our job to establish a new advanced OSS base in Sian, which is in Northwest China near the lower bend of the Yellow River. From Sian a new secret ground war and intelligence apparatus in North China was to be launched.

The Fourteenth Air Force had an advanced air base in Sian, and a large volume of supplies was being flown from Kunming and Chengtu over the mountains to Sian. However, the Fourteenth never had enough gasoline, food, and munitions. It was always generous with OSS, relations between the two organizations being excellent. But OSS had to augment its supplies by carrying them overland.

The distance from Kunming to Sian by the only available roads was about fifteen hundred miles. Approximately halfway between the two cities was Chengtu. Here, and at Chanyi, about a hundred miles from Kunming, it was possible to secure extra gasoline and a few spare parts for vehicles. Otherwise, convoys on this route were on their own. They had to be self-sufficient in every way up to the last days of the war when the Army Service of Supply made available emergency supplies of gasoline and parts at two intermediate points.

The only existing serviceable maps had been made by exploratory groups of American army engineers, and these were not like American road maps. Each party that went through was likely to discover for itself gaps in the published information. The country was generally high, rugged, and lonely. Some of the men who made the trip claimed they counted twenty-one major mountain ranges. Except for the Red Basin in Szechwan and a few narrow valleys, there was little level land.

I was lucky to be on the first OSS convoy to make the trip. Later I took a large group of vehicles through myself. The following is a composite account based on both convoys. It pictures a China relatively few Americans have seen. It may indicate why so many Americans who have traveled in the interior of China love the land and its people. The fact that such a convoy route could be established was to the credit of the Chungking government; ten years earlier these roads had not existed.

I was particularly interested in the northern two-thirds of this country because it was the homeland of the Ko Lao Hui, the Society of Elder Brothers. Mr. Chen had put me under the protection of this society and given me its password. This was Mr. Chen's China.

It was a cold summer morning in the high plateau

of Kunming. The rain was sweeping in translucent sheets across the land, filling the ditches with yellow water, and rushing in torrents down the red gullies on the mountains. Twenty trucks were lined up on the Burma Road waiting for the signal to start. We were anxious to make a good record for there has been trouble on practically all previous convoys with trucks breaking down, running out of gas, or going off cliffs.

We were heavily armed, each officer and man carrying at least two weapons of his own choice ready for immediate action. We had no intention of surrendering our valuable cargo to anyone; the men had been ordered to fight to the finish if necessary, but to invite no trouble. They were fine men, full of oats after months of sitting around various headquarters and replacement depots. Some of the boys had celebrated far too well the previous night and were hardly in the pink of condition, but we rounded them up and got on our way. For miles we passed through U.S. military establishments of various types. Then the road climbed to the hills which rim the Kunming Valley.

This was wild country, miles of barren land producing only tall grasses and scrub pines. We were wet and miserable, for a chill breeze carried the rain. The altitude was about nine thousand feet. There were many petty breakdowns and annoyances. The radios in my jeep, which led the convoy, and that of Captain Bill Weiss, my executive, who was bringing up the rear, were soaked and refused to function. It was hard to keep the vehicles together without the help of radio communication between the two ends of the convoy.

When we reached the top of the first pass and started

downhill, I stepped on my brake pedal and discovered I had no brakes. By good luck, I was able to steer off the road on a level spot and stop. Someone in our OSS motor pool had cut a fibre tube which carried brake fluid so the brakes would be sure to go when they were most needed. This was a small but typical act of sabotage. I wondered how many Americans in our war had died this way. I had to drive all day with no brakes. Repairs were made that night at the air force base at Chanyi.

About forty miles out of Kunming, we felt that we had gotten rid of the bugs and were rolling along as a unit. We had fallen into a routine. As we skirted the side of a valley, I noticed that my radio operator, Jack Kilby, the other passenger in my jeep, had fallen asleep with his head bent over his knees. I was sleepy myself.

Suddenly a bullet whipped past the back of my neck. I had the impression it might have gotten Jack if he had been sitting up straight. It was hard to believe that anyone was actually shooting at us, but my momentary doubt was removed when another bullet ricocheted off the road in front of me. I could either stop the convoy, order the men into the ditches, and fight it out, or try to run the gauntlet. The road was good so I chose to run for it since the firing was coming from trees several hundred yards above us. The fact that I had no brakes didn't give me much choice. We were lucky and suffered no losses.

A few days later, another OSS convoy at approximately the same spot was fired on, and my friend Major Philip Crowe saw a hole suddenly appear in the top of his jeep. He stopped, jumped out with a tommy gun, and sprayed the hillside. Six men emerged from hiding several hundred yards away and ran off safely.

There are two schools of thought about whether a convoy should stop, or go ahead, when it is fired on; my men were instructed to keep going as long as they could, to stay together under all circumstances, and to close in fast with weapons ready if they saw that any vehicle ahead of them had been held up.

Farther along the road, we came to a place long famous for bandits. Here the Chinese army had taken over and were patrolling the pass through which the road descends to the Chanyi Valley. There were a series of fortified houses built high above the road from which bandits formerly spied out the land to descend on chosen objectives. But troops in battle dress, trained and equipped by Americans, riding in American jeeps, had made banditry unpopular and the convoys shuttled through the gorge with impunity except for an occasional potshot.

There was a large American airfield at Chanyi which was also at the end of a railroad from Kunming. This was a busy supply center and a base for bombers and fighters operating against the Japanese. There was a transient camp operated by the Service of Supply, SOS as it was known to the troops, but this time it was crowded and we had to go on our way after gassing up and fixing my brakes.

We stopped for the night in an abandoned field opposite an ammunition dump. We all had cots, jungle hammocks, ponchos, and plenty of bedding. The jungle hammock is a remarkable invention, a combined tent and mosquito net and hammock. When it is slung between trucks, and rests on a cot, it provides good sleeping.

There was a soldier in the convoy whose name, Tony Rosofsky, I will ever bless. He was a junior executive in a rubber company in Ohio before the war. At this time he was a private and one of the most competent, energetic men I can remember working with. After driving a heavy truck over vile roads all day, he would officiate as a cook. From cartons of Ten-in-One rations, with the help of a field range, he prepared a fine supper. He cooked for us the whole time we were on the road. And when the help of an extra mechanic was needed, he volunteered to work on a broken spring late into the night.

There were many fine people in OSS. The greatest strength of the organization was that it attracted so many outstanding men. Robert Chappelet was a case in point. On my first trip over the Sian road, we rode together in a weapons carrier, together with a valiant young French-Jewish lieutenant, Michel Block, who escaped from France during the occupation, joined DeGaulle, transferred to OSS, and eventually became an American citizen and a lieutenant in the American army.

Robert Chappelet was born in Switzerland in a family of wealthy wine merchants. Bob might have led a placid, comfortable life, but while he was a young man, he seems to have received a kind of Pauline revelation. He is a devout Catholic, a kind of monk without vows, a Rabelaisian but devout Christian, full of contradictions, and a fine human being.

Bob's international adventures began when he became interested in training dogs while serving as a conscript in the Swiss army. He was so successful he was invited to go to America to teach Americans to train Seeing Eye dogs. He worked in New Jersey until he got bored, then returned to Switzerland where he became a practical architect.

He heard that the Order of St. Bernard planned to build a monastery high in the Himalayas on the border between China and Tibet, so he volunteered for the job. He served for eight years without pay, designing the building, recruiting and training labor among the aborigines, superintending construction, making friends everywhere. He bought a small farm in the valley below the pass, and was happy.

All men were equal in Chappelet's eyes, and he was the boon companion of a collection of fantastic people. The chief of the Lisu tribe in the nearby mountains looked on him with favor because he effected some amazing cures with European drugs. Bob doctored his friends because their misery was so great. He relied heavily on injections of mercury and arsenic since he assumed rightly that most of the maladies he saw around him were venereal. His patients were fortunately able to absorb doses that might kill a European.

Bob collected the mythology of the tribesmen of the Tibetan borderland. He learned their languages, became their champion against the Chinese who preempted the good farms of the valley floors, and forced the Lisu and other tribesmen into the mountains. After eight years among these primitive peoples, he heard of the great war with Japan. He decided that the duty of a Christian was to help defeat the Japanese. He had little money, was a citizen of a neutral country, but he decided to walk over the Himalayas through Burma to India where he would offer his services to the British.

Bob bought a lot of salt which was plentiful where he lived but in great demand along his prospective route. He rounded up some of his friends to carry the salt and his few belongings. It was midwinter and the high passes were snowbound. For fourteen days Bob and his friends struggled through the snow, over passes as high as the peaks of the Rockies and the Alps. Two of his men died of cold and hardships, but finally Bob reached Fort Hertz in the northern tip of Burma. There he sold the remaining salt, paid his surviving men handsomely, and had enough profit to carry him to Calcutta.

The British were cautious about hiring him. They made him many promises but he got tired of waiting for them to be kept. Then he was invited to join the Americans in OSS. Later he was assigned to a project to which I was attached. Since he spoke eight Oriental languages, he could have been very valuable if he had been given a chance to serve. Like many others, he was embalmed in red tape for many months until his patience wore thin. On this convoy he was on the open road again and was like a colt in a green pasture.

Bob carried with him a store of Pax Brandy made by the Catholic fathers in Kunming, and with this pleasant remedy he strengthened morale on various occasions. He would also break in with preposterous stories to improve the moral atmosphere. His store of such tales seemed endless.

One day someone complained about the characteristic Chinese cruelty to animals. Bob said that the Lisu attitude was a marked contrast to that of the Chinese and illustrated his point. There was a certain Lisu tribe which suffered periodically from a plague of monkeys which raided their fields. The Lisu are a gentle people who have been taught not to take the lives of animals. So they built a big trap in the form of a corncrib, with bamboo sides and plenty of space between each vertical stake. The monkeys discovered this treasure grove and, suspecting nothing, were soon all inside eating their fill whereupon the watching Lisu pulled a string which closed the door.

The whole tribe then gathered around the trap. Instead of killing the monkeys, they stuck poles between the bamboo slats and proceeded to beat them almost to death. There were terror and pandemonium inside the trap. Some of the monkeys might die but that would be accidental. Eventually the door was opened and the survivors ran like deer. They told their friends what happened to them and for a long time these Lisu people were not bothered by monkeys, all because they were kind to animals.

Later Chappelet served with distinction behind the enemy lines in Honan and was there when the war ended. He was there when the Chinese "rescuing" troops entered a city a few hours after the Japanese left. The Chinese troops started a reign of terror worse than the people had ever known under the Japanese. This continued until the Chinese commander stopped it and told his men he was ashamed of them. Chappelet in another age might have been a knight or a saint. He was a very perfect, gentle soldier.

Near Chanyi we met some of Stilwell's Chinese troops who had been flown up from Burma to stop the Japanese if they tried to advance up the Chanyi Valley. They were impressive soldiers compared to others we had seen in the Chinese army. They were strong, well-nourished men, proud of their calling. Not far beyond one of their camps we saw another type of soldier lying face up at the edge of the road. He was dead. He was one of many such whom we saw, dead or barely alive, who had been turned out of their units sick or wounded.

The United States Army taught its men in China that it was not safe to drink any unboiled water or to eat Chinese food. We were told that disease was rampant, that we would be lucky to escape it, and then only if we quarantined ourselves against it by scrupulously refraining from any unnecessary contacts with the Chinese people. This was mainly ridiculous. There are countless streams in the mountains of China fit for swimming and countless springs for drinking. As for Chinese food, it is superb.

On my first convoy our commanding officer, a reserve major, was a North Carolina schoolteacher, who had read a book which convinced him that all water in China is polluted. We were ordered, under no circumstances, to drink unboiled water. We ran out of Kunming water on the second day while climbing through a pine forest to a high pass. The major halted the convoy on a small clearing where a big spring of ice-cold water gushed from the rocks. He ordered one man to build a stone fireplace and start a fire. Another man was ordered to bring out a filthy GI garbage can, wash it, fill it with water, and place it over the fire. Unfortunately, the soft solder on the bottom of the can melted; the bottom fell out and the water drowned the fire. The major said nothing; he started off in his jeep leaving us by the spring. We filled our canteens and followed.

There were several officers on this convoy who had sworn they would not touch Chinese food. One night we stopped at a little town called Suanwei, across a wild, pine-clad plateau from Chanyi. An elderly Chinese gentleman told Bob Chappelet and me that this town was famous for fine ham. He also told us where to find a first-class restaurant. We strolled off toward the city gate and some of the avowed abstainers trailed along to see what would happen. We were disobeying the standing orders of our major. He had told us he would prefer charges against anyone who ate Chinese food.

Bob spoke superb vernacular Chinese and between the two of us, we persuaded the restaurant keeper to give us his best. He produced a clean tablecloth (it had been left behind ten years earlier by an American naturalist), and set on it a great bowl of boiling water. In this we dipped our chopsticks, spoons, and bowls. Then came a procession of dishes. The food and wine were magnificent. The doubters took a nibble and a drink apiece and were converted. It was a memorable meal. We were all full of good cheer when we heard military boots on the cobblestones. In came our commanding officer who drew up an extra chair, sat down without a word, and ate and drank until he, too, was full. Some of the finest eating in the world is to be found in out-of-the-way places in China. Suanwei was near oak forests where pigs grew fat on acorns and produced great hams which were cured over fragrant smoke. In the woods were wild fruits, including the Chinese *Arbutus,* which produces a fine, dry, red wine. Considering the climate, the scenery, and the food, several of us would have been content to stay in this valley until the end of the war.

After that night our commander and the other men who had sworn not to eat Chinese food, because the Chinese are so dirty, tried to camp each night near a town so they could have a good meal instead of K-rations. They had learned a valuable lesson which helped to make their lives easier and happier in the remote interior of China. Proper indoctrination of its men by the American army should have included schooling in how to live comfortably and safely in a strange land. This would have helped both the Americans and the Chinese.

There is a secluded valley in the high mountains of western Kweichow province which I shall always remember with a special happiness. It is not a particularly impressive spot. It might be any valley in the lower Rockies, or even in the Adirondacks. You reach this valley after traversing many miles of dangerous road. The highway rises from Suanwei into forested mountains, and for a half day the trucks swim around dangerous curves cut out of cliffs or squarely on top of sharp ridges where a mistake would send the vehicle and its contents hurtling down hundreds of feet.

In these mountains there are aborigines. The Lolos are a fierce people who had never been conquered by the Chinese. (I have often wondered how they fared under the government of Mao Tse-tung.) They are divided into three castes: Black Bones, White Bones, and slaves. The Black Bones are the aristocracy, the pureblooded Lolos. Their business is war. The White Bones are an intermediate class and represent the offspring of mixed marriages. The slaves are Chinese and members of other tribes, such as the Miaos and, at that time, reportedly a few Americans who had bailed out of wounded airplanes.

The Lolos I saw were professional warriors, an erect, proud people. Their cooperation had been purchased by the Chinese so that we sometimes saw groups of them patrolling the road. Their rifles were always well oiled, in contrast to the weapons of the average Chinese soldier.

We were held up at one point by a broken-down truck, and I had a chance to buy a Lolo fighting dagger in a black lacquer scabbard. It was a beautiful weapon. It was later captured by Chinese Communists together with most of the curiosities I had collected as a soldier.

We camped in a meadow above a clear stream in my valley. We were fearful of attack for it was a region famous for bandits. It rained hard that night. I ditched the ground around a trailer and slept under it quite comfortably. We had posted guards and all of us had our weapons ready. The only disturbance I suffered was from two Americans who had paid seven thousand Chinese dollars for a tough old hen (a fabulous price even in American money) and who were determined to eat it. They had built a campfire, but the meat would not get tender. While they were waiting, they consoled themselves with a bottle of Pax Brandy. Soon they had forgotten both the chicken and the rain. The last I saw of them before I went to sleep, they were huddled there together by the dying fire, speaking solemnly of grave subjects, with the bottle between them.

The last time we stayed in this spot was after we had had some trouble with a Chinese major who had wrecked his vehicle against one of our trucks. The fault was clearly his, but he had been furious and I was afraid we might be attacked that night. We mounted two machine guns to command the approaches and had no trouble.

Then, with daylight, came the poor Miao farmers to pick up tin cans and sell us eggs. They were poor beyond belief. They have handsome tribal costumes, but the Chinese have discouraged the wearing of the beautiful garments. Our visitors were cringing and woebegone. They were the kicked-around descendants of people who had been abused for two thousand years.

There was a strange bond between Chappelet and all children, and all simple, oppressed peoples. These included all the tribesmen we met, even the Lolos, who have done very well for themselves on their great fourteen-thousand-feet-high fortress of a plateau. He had a special affinity for the Lisu, perhaps because he had once loved an eighteen-year-old Lisu girl, the daughter of a chief, who had been the most beautiful girl he had ever seen. She died while he was away on a trip.

Beyond this valley the mountains rose steeply, and the road climbed for the first time beyond the heavy timber into the grasslands. Here the Lisu lived in crude huts built like American tepees out of branches. They wore filthy white felt cloaks and herded sheep and a few small cattle among the hyacinths and azaleas of their high prairies.

There are in China many millions of non-Chinese people. This means usually that their ancestors lived in China before the Chinese arrived. On the other hand, the Mohammedans in the Northwest are descendants of men who arrived after the migrations of the first Chinese. Besides the tribes that have been mentioned are such people as the Hakka in the Southeast, the Moi in Yunnan, the Chiarong tribes of the Tibetan borderland, and the pathetic Chiangs (once a great people, now being pushed to oblivion).

The Chinese Nationalist attitude toward this large minority population was much like the traditional American attitude toward the Indians. We are hardly in a position to criticize, but the Chinese have traditionally treated these peoples with tyrannical harshness. The various Moslem groups have responded by a fierce hatred which periodically blossoms into bitter war. The Lolos also are great warriors and have the advantage of living in a remote wilderness. Some of the more inoffensive aboriginal peoples seemed close to extermination.

The Chinese seem to have made precisely the same mistakes we have made in dealing with our minorities. The Chinese approached these primitive peoples with an unshakable assurance of their own superiority. They seemed to find it impossible to deal with the tribesmen as equals. This is particularly true if by chance the tribesmen are a hairy people with generous beards. The Chinese have been taught for generations that the more hair a man has the closer he is to the savage.

Peking claims to have adopted a new, humane policy toward its minorities. I hope so. Some of these peoples possess proud traditions. The great engineer, Li P'ing, who designed the irrigation system of the Chengtu plain two thousand years ago was a Chiang. Many so-called primitives have made important contributions to Chinese civilization. They should all be welcomed as equals, permitted to preserve their own cultures, while adopting the best of Chinese tradition.

Twenty-five years ago, the Miao, with their quaint customs, their love of music and dancing, were rapidly becoming second-rate Chinese, distinguishable from other Chinese chiefly by their greater poverty. Their wonderful costumes, hand-embroidered and passed on from mother to daughter, in which their young women flitted like butterflies along the mountain roads, were rapidly disappearing and were being replaced by the drab Chinese indigo peasant clothing.

American convoys were frequently molested by both uniformed troops and civilians in 1944–45. Sometimes a number of bandits in plain clothes, with their weapons under their coats, clustered innocently in the road. When a bus or truck approached, the guns would appear and the shooting would start.

We encountered several suspicious looking groups. Sometimes the weapons they had were clearly visible. However, we had an antidote which never failed. The leading jeep would slow down and all the other vehicles would close up behind it. Men would stand on the running boards with tommy guns in their hands, and the general effect was of a porcupine ready for battle. The highwaymen always grinned and waved us on our way.

I was leading one convoy as we approached a pass at about twelve thousand feet. I saw sunlight reflected on gunmetal among the pines which flanked the pass a few hundred yards ahead of us. The convoy stopped and we had target practice for about ten minutes, firing weapons ranging from pistols to heavy machine guns and a bazooka. About fifty Lolo tribesmen left their ambush and clapped for us as we nervously crawled up the pass between them.

There are many lakes among the mountains, and the loveliest of these is at Weining. Here the road comes down briefly from the mountains to an altitude of seventy-five hundred feet and skirts one side of a fine sheet of water that reminded me of Lake Tahoe. But it was not so pretty as Tahoe because around it was a fringe of farmland and the people along the road were poor and dispirited. In winter and spring, the lake was heavily populated with wild ducks and geese and swan. The air was crisp and clean, and the breeze carried the muffled conversation of a

host of wild fowl. The city of Weining seems to have been
originally a frontier fortress. The walls were still formidable. Refugees had poured into this pioneer land and
there were many new schools; at noon the road was lined
by pretty, clean, little schoolgirls in their prescribed costumes and boys looking very military in their Sun Yat-sen
uniforms.

North of Weining the road climbs almost continuously for twenty miles. There is a high pass in the grasslands populated only by a few primitive tribesmen. Here
we halted for a rest and to see the view, a superb pano-
rama of tumbled mountains. The men were encouraged
to indulge in target practice for the sound of the guns
would travel far and wide, and warn any gentlemen with
evil inclinations to think twice before molesting us. So the
high, thin air echoed with machine gun and rifle fire and
the explosion of grenades and bazooka rockets.

The plateau here begins to be cut by deep valleys and
the streams flow north toward the Yangtze. From the pass
the road descended steadily for many miles into the first
of a series of subtropical valleys. The road was narrow
and the grades were steep. It was a dangerous highway,
particularly in winter. There were a number of American
army trucks lying in the bottom of a gorge far below us.
I heard of one truck loaded with TNT which slid off and
landed some fifteen hundred feet below in the bed of a
stream. By some miracle the crew got out safely and there
was no explosion.

We found it oppressively hot in the valley and were
glad to reach the next mountain where the road was cut
out of the side of a precipitous slope above a natural
bridge. The pass here was one of the highest and most

beautiful of the entire route. Near the highest point was a meadow full of wild hyacinths and ripe strawberries. Here we camped in the mild afternoon sunlight.

It was pleasant to lie in the tall grass among the purple hyacinths and pick the small, fragrant berries. The men were like boys let out of school. As soon as the trucks were parked and serviced, the machine guns mounted, and their cots set up, they began to frolic. Some of them hunted the pheasants that were calling on the slopes about us. Others gathered wood for a bonfire. These were helped by a family of stunted apelike primitives who lived in a huge cave nearby and cultivated sweet potatoes.

Sunset was very beautiful, an alpine glow momentarily touching the distant blue peaks before they faded into the night. We were perched on a rim of a huge, dead, volcanic crater which was surrounded by steeplelike pinnacles. The air was thin, keen, and sweet. The men had trampled the grass and crushed many ripe berries so that the meadow was covered by pungent fragrance.

Two of the men were having birthdays, and Tony, the cook, celebrated the occasion by preparing a fine supper. We ate hugely and basked in lazy quietness. To celebrate the birthdays, I gave each man a half canteen cup of the fine brandy we had bought from the French fathers in Kunming. The darkness fell quickly and the men clustered about the fire talking and laughing. Then a cloud settled on the mountain and we were wrapped in fog. Except for the men on guard everyone went to bed.

Here rank carried few privileges. Contrary to common military practice, all officers including the one in command stood guard in their turn, a custom supported by everyone except one officer. A young lieutenant, just

out from Washington, told me it was contrary to regulations; therefore he refused to stand watch. He changed
his mind.

During my two hours of watch, a cold rain fell
through the fog. We had trouble keeping the fire alive but
managed to heat some water for coffee. The wind and the
inpenetrable blackness had transformed the friendly
meadow and had surrounded us with potential hostility.
By morning the meadow was a quagmire.

The valley, thousands of feet below the pass, looked
like Yosemite. Here there was extensive rice cultivation,
which meant that we were approaching the level of the
Yangtze. The first time I saw this valley, it was on a clear
spring evening when the high surrounding peaks were
glowing with rose-colored light. The great cliffs towering
above it looked as though they had been painted by Max-
field Parrish.

At a small city called Pichieh, there was a mission
operated by German Lutheran Sisters. The chief of these
was Sister Margaret whose hospitality was not limited by
nationality or hampered by war. She made a practice of
feeding all passing American troops. She and her helpers
were the most popular people on the road. She told me
she had fed more than fifteen hundred American soldiers.
We were technically enemies. We found Sister Margaret
one morning after a very difficult night. She provided us
a place to wash and a huge breakfast. All of us contributed to a collection to support her work.

There was a tremendous canyon beyond Pichieh. It
was comparable to the gorge of the Salween on the Burma
Road or the Grand Canyon of the Colorado. We reached
it late in the afternoon. The road descended precipitiously

for ten miles, switching back and forth along the steep mountain, and finally flattened out on the bed of the river in air that smelled like a hothouse. First we tried to camp on a gravel spit by the river, but one of the trucks bogged down. We snaked out and crossed the bridge into the little town that rose on a series of terraces on the opposite mountain. We found a hospitable welcome in the compound of the Chinese government motor pool.

The Chihshui River made a constant music in the bottom of the gorge, and the air was sluggish after the keen air of the highlands. Bananas and oranges were for sale here, a welcome addition to our rations. There was a sandbar near the motor pool around which the clean, blue water swept in an arc. The men who weren't too tired got out their towels and went there after dark to bathe. I was asleep when they returned but awoke to overhear them tell their friends what had happened. A number of village girls had stolen down the quiet streets to join them by the edge of the river. It is the only time I ever heard of village girls doing such a thing. However, local customs vary greatly. I heard a large, tough soldier say, "My girl was so beautiful. She was so lovely."

The road ascended again into the cold upper air. It wound in and out of jumbled mountain tops, through prosperous villages, approaching the Yangtze. Finally it came to the jumping-off place where it suddenly dropped several thousand feet down the face of a mountain in a series of twenty-seven sharp switchbacks. At the foot of the mountain, the road entered a gorge with high, perpendicular walls and a fine clear stream which at home would have had trout. We stopped here to fish with grenades. The men stripped and hid behind boulders while grenades were exploded in the deep water. Soon fish began to belly up, and the men dove in to get them. We had a large audience of country people, and most of the fish went to them. They were delighted to receive such fine gifts. Our best haul, in several attempts, was twelve large mountain carp from one pool. They probably averaged two feet in length. We gave these to a Catholic orphanage in the next town.

This same gorge was the scene of a curious adventure one night. A convoy had run short of gas farther back in the mountains, and one jeep was going ahead to hunt for gasoline. As the jeep swung around a corner of the cliff, it had to slow down to avoid running into a large, striped animal which had apparently been drinking at the stream. The driver was a young lieutenant who began to admire the fine Great Dane dog he had so unexpectedly encountered. But the "dog" turned around to look at the headlights, and the amazed lieutenant suddenly realized he was looking at a tiger. There was a soldier sleeping in the back seat, and when the driver had succeeded in awakening him, the tiger was loping along at a good speed looking for a place to get off the road. Just as he found it, the passenger let loose a blast from a tommy gun, and the tiger jumped off the road. They did not stop to investigate.

The new highway crosses the Yangtze at Luhsien. Here was a typical booming interior city, little known even in China. If the war had lasted a year longer, Luhsien might have become better known, even outside China; an immense concrete air base had been built here to handle larger and heavier freight planes than those which operated on the Hump and runs to Chengtu and Kunming.

We saw this airfield as it was being finished. Unnumbered thousands of men, women, and children were carrying dirt in little baskets, doing a dozen jobs under American supervision. Thus they quickly created a broad belt of glistening concrete about two miles long on the bank of the river.

All around the field were the camps built for the American personnel who were beginning to arrive when the war ended. It was to have been a big establishment, but was stillborn. I speculated on how much American money was wasted on this one project; also, I have often wondered how long it took for the local farmers to tear up all that beautiful concrete to recreate the lost paddy fields. A more likely probability is that the Luhsien base is now being used by Mao's air force.

It was clear that the Americans in Luhsien were not popular. In the country, along the road, we invariably were treated with extreme courtesy and a rich, spontaneous friendliness, but not here. The American soldiers had quickly worn out their welcome.

Including the Yangtze, there are three rivers to be crossed in a distance of about sixty miles. Crossing a river with a convoy in China is a major operation. The ferries are small barges which generally accommodate at most two trucks at a time. If the water is wide, there may be an antiquated steam launch to haul the barge. Usually, there is nothing more than manpower available. If this manpower is feeling sullen or uncooperative, you are stuck.

At one ferry there was a large Chinese convoy which had been held up for nearly twenty-four hours. The ferry was not running. They were all government operated, and legally free, but some of the managers liked to collect a little graft on the side. I talked to the leader of the Chinese trucks and he said I could try to get across the river ahead of his vehicles. He grinned as he spoke and obviously did not think I would have much luck. I gave him some American cigarettes and a couple of dollars worth of Chinese currency and began our campaign.

There was a Chinese college boy interpreter with us with the rank of major. I explained the situation to him and he was happy to cooperate. He hired a sampan to carry him across to the opposite ferry landing. As soon as I saw him talking to the ferry manager, I walked down to the water's edge and began to fire my .45 slowly into the water. There were hills on either side of the river and the sound echoed awesomely through the morning mist.

My ambassador informed the ferry manager that I would keep on shooting until the ferry started to operate, that I would slowly raise the muzzle of my pistol toward him until he would be under fire. There was a flurry of activity and the ferry was on its way to our side of the river. After we were across we discovered that the manager was an expatriate, like myself, from Foochow on the China coast. He was delighted to hear someone, especially a foreigner, speak his native tongue. I gave him a generous bribe of cigarettes and money and we parted friends.

We had very little trouble at any time with thieves. In the country, where the population was unchanged by contacts with foreigners, they were as honest as any people. However, they became corrupted by contact with Americans. The last ferry was famous for pickpockets, and the men were warned to be on guard. There were swarms of attractive urchins who sold peanuts and hard-boiled eggs and stole anything they could lay their hands on. They made a good haul in spite of our precautions. Among other treasures, they got a hand grenade out of a glove compartment. I hate to think of what probably happened when they experimented with their new treasure.

Now we were crossing the Red Basin of Szechwan, a region of rolling hills and fertile plains, one of the granaries of China. It is a rich and lovely land. At one point we had halted for temporary repairs when I overheard a conversation between a Chinese colonel and a well-dressed man and woman. They were walking past our vehicles. The colonel said, "Don't touch anything belonging to the Americans. They think we are all thieves, and shoot first and ask questions afterward." Even the prettiest farming country tends to become dull. Aside from a few potshots that someone hidden in an orchard took at us, nothing happened of interest.

After a few days rest at the OSS camp near Chengtu, called Camp Oasis, we were again on our way, and for a day we bounced over the fertile Chengtu plain. This was summertime and the sun was hot, yet there was a fresh tang of the mountains in the air. A few miles away to the west rose the first high wall of Tibet.

In the mountains we generally could find a good campsite, but in the cultivated lowlands it was not so easy. One time we hunted in vain for a place to stay, at a town called Mienyang, Valley of Cotton. Finally, we were invited into the compound of a mission school. When our hosts discovered that the gate was too low, they tore out the sill. They worked hard to make it possible for us to find shelter for the night, and next morning they must have had a half-day's work repairing the damage they had done to their gate on our behalf.

Beyond Mienyang, the road again takes to the

mountains. For several hundred miles it follows periodically the old Imperial Tribute Highway, which for many centuries was one of the principal trade routes of central Asia. During the Tang dynasty, over a thousand years ago, an emperor had ordered that young *Cryptomerias* be planted along this road. The *Cryptomeria*, also called the Japan Cedar, is a great tree. It reaches a venerable age and huge proportions. These trees were protected by an ancient superstition according to which anyone who destroyed one would come to a bad end. It was probably more than a superstition in the days when the empire flourished.

This is the tree which sometimes grows in fine groves around old monasteries. It is associated with antiquity, religious establishments, and tombs. It is one of the most beautiful trees I have ever seen. The old, stone-flagged highway winds in and out through the valleys and over the mountains, and is marked as far as the eye can reach by the protecting double column of great *Cryptomerias*. At the top of the first pass, there was a dense grove of *Cryptomerias* surrounding an imposing red monastery. Temples have a certain sanctity about them which sometimes has spared them the destruction of the wars that have ravaged China for thousands of years.

I halted our caravan in the shade of the old trees and told the men they might inspect the monastery. It turned out to be a monument to some obscure hero of the Han dynasty who had flourished at about the time of Christ. It was in excellent condition and contained a set of mural paintings which were extraordinarily fine. These, according to a scholarly monk, were more than a thousand years old. They should have been in a museum. The flowers and murals were beginning to deteriorate, and the delicate princesses in their gardens were beginning to be blurred by time.

According to the air force map which we had been given before we started, there were no mountains in an area which we found full of fine, wild ranges. Maps of China, especially of the interior, were very imperfect during World War II.

Amidst these nonexistent mountains, we found an ideal camping place on a gravel bank above a river. Here we were alone, with no dwellings near and no shelter for anyone who might feel inclined to sneak up on our camp. We arranged our vehicles in a circle, each one pointing out like the spokes of a wheel. In the middle, we built a bonfire and had supper. The river swept with a continuous whispering in a half circle around us. The water had lately been acquainted with glaciers and snowfields in the high Tsinglings, but this did not deter us from bathing in a stinging cold lagoon.

After dark there was a heavy dew and a great peacefulness. I remember thinking that this is what men remember after a war, the quiet nights under the stars, the fellowship, the feeling that one is part of something big and worthwhile. It is such memories that seduce one into forgetting the organized boredom of military life and all the manifold stupidities of armies.

Someone began to signal with a flashlight from a farmhouse on a mountain across the river. He was answered by someone else at the ferry we had just crossed. This went on for some time, and it seemed reasonable to assume that we were the subject of this conversation. Our guards were strengthened, but nothing happened to spoil the peace of the starlight.

The road north of Chengtu generally reaches no

great altitudes because it follows river valleys and crosses low passes. The scenery is superb and if that country were in America, it would be dotted with tourist resorts. One pass is actually an immense natural bridge. A sizable river flows underground for about two miles. This is a great country, built on a massive scale. Where the stream goes under the mountain, there is a black cave, at least one hundred and fifty feet high, in a cliff that towers hundreds of feet above the bed of the river. To an amateur geologist, it appears that the whole valley was once a vast cavern and that the top has caved in everywhere except at this one place.

The rivers in this country flow through canyons, and there is often no room for a road, so the Chinese engineers blasted ledges out of the rock. Our truck rumbled along on a narrow strip of roadway with a roof of solid rock overhead. In some places an error in judgment could send the vehicle flying hundreds of feet into the foaming water far below. It is a country of clear water. There are pools like crystal where small fish play in the shallows. There are long ripples of white water, where the water flows out in the open sunlight and makes rainbows as it falls over the ledge on its way to the rocks in the bottom of the gorge.

There is a plain in these mountains which is one of the oldest cradles of Chinese civilization. It is watered by crystalline rivers. The land rises and falls like the prairies of America. It is walled by fine peaks. Here, for the first time, one meets North China, which is something quite unlike the China of the South and of the Yangtze Valley. The chief town in this plain is Hanchung. Here there was a large American air base where one night we found shelter. The Japanese once hoped to take Hanchung but were defeated by the Fourteenth Air Force, and perhaps also by their own indecision and poor leadership.

The exit from the plain is through a superb gorge. The road is cut out of the mountain and follows a beautiful stream which has a succession of spacious pools connected by swift, white water. This valley leads to the main pass through the Tsingling Mountains, which form a wall running across China from west to east for a thousand miles. When the weather was cool, there were many columns of camels on this road. These were the heavily furred Mongolian variety; they were the chief means of transportation in this area as they had been for thousands of years. Each man in a caravan had five camels to control. They were afraid of motorcars and were always led to the side of the road and turned to face approaching vehicles. Otherwise, they stampeded wildly. When they were too tired or sick to carry their burden, they simply lay down and died beside the road and were eaten by their masters and by dogs and wolves.

Where the gorge reaches the high mountains, it widens out a bit, and there are pockets of rolling land along the river which are cultivated. In one such valley is a magnificent stone fort, evidently built by a first-class military engineer, possibly Genghis Khan. Before the introduction of modern artillery, it might have been impregnable. It appeared to be deserted. I could learn nothing of its history. On a late summer evening long ago, it looked like an enchanted fortress.

A regular stop for American convoys was Miaotaisze, a hamlet tucked away in a pine forest at the foot of the high backbone of the mountains. Here there was a superb

Taoist temple alleged to be some two thousand years old. There were some thatched sheds built to protect the camel and mule caravans that frequented the road. Here we parked our trucks, washed in the ice water that raced past us in three separate brooks, and went to the monastery for supper. The China Travel Service operated a hotel in part of the monastery. The food was excellent.

A goodly proportion of the population of this isolated village were refugees, and some of them were poor. Chappelet immediately made friends with the children, and pampered them until they were a nuisance, everlastingly scrounging for food, for empty tins, and for anything they could lay their hands on. I noticed a wan little girl who did not join in the scrambling after gifts, so I called her over to me and gave her several cans of food and some sugar from K-rations. She thanked me like a grand old lady.

"What are you called?" I asked her.

"My name is Wu," she replied.

After that I watched for her and called her by name to give her whatever I could give away. When I returned several months later, she recognized me with a shy smile. She had grown thinner, and I thought she might either have tuberculosis or be slowly starving to death. Her manners were still those of a fine lady.

There was much game in those mountains. In about three hours one morning, four men shot twenty-five pheasants. We saw some deer occasionally along the road, and the people said tigers and leopards were fairly common.

The monastery was used for a time as a rest camp by the Army Air Force personnel stationed at Hanchung.

miraculous event was reported. Workmen digging near the Wei River, at the place where the road from the great Tsingling pass meets the river, had found a lump of gold shaped like a chicken. This, according to the soothsayers, was a very good omen, so the new city was built where the chicken had been found and was called Paochi, the Precious Chicken.

Much more recently Paochi became the inland terminus of a railroad from the ocean. The French builders of this road intended to extend it into Kansu and, later, all the way to Turkestan to connect with Russian lines. It had never been completed, but it had done much for the people who lived along its thousand miles of track. According to reports from Peking, the Communist regime has extended this railroad hundreds of miles to the west and opened vast new areas for farming and industry.

Sian is about one hundred and fifty miles east of Paochi. There were two ways to take a convoy from one city to the other. The first and safest was to drive the trucks onto flatcars and let a locomotive pull you to Sian. It took about twenty-four hours and was a trying experience. The engine drowned you with soot. The train was maddeningly slow. We had to harden our heart and prevent poor travelers from climbing on our trucks. If we took any, we had to take all; so the only safe thing to do was to take none. The other way to take trucks from Paochi to Sian was to drive them over the primitive loess highway. This was passable in dry weather but when it rained one sat tight wherever he was until the road was dry again.

When I was commanding the convoy, we were in

a hurry to get the supplies we were carrying to Sian, and we would have had to wait perhaps a week to travel by train. The weather in the west looked bad but we decided to gamble. It was an interesting trip through the heart of one of the richest loess regions. We passed through several cities which certainly had not seen many Americans. The gates were too low for the biggest trucks so they had to lower their tops to get through. All this time, the rain was pursuing us across this high, rolling tableland.

We saw the first indication that Sian was near when we stopped to rest briefly near the pyramid of a Chou dynasty emperor. The plateau near Sian is liberally sprinkled with such tombs, some of them comparing favorably in size with the great pyramids of Egypt. Then on the horizon appeared the crenellated wall and the magnificent city gates of Sian.

We heard the roaring of a squadron of fighters taking off to attack the Japanese on the other side of the Yellow River, about ten minutes flying time away. We were home. We had traveled fifteen hundred miles in twelve traveling days and had arrived with one broken spring and one flat tire among twenty trucks. We had brought many tons of urgently needed supplies. It was an insignificant routine operation but the men were as proud as veterans of a great battle.

My commanding officer, Major Krause, a friend I had first met in India, showed me a copy of a radiogram he sent to OSS headquarters in Kunming. He commended me for bringing the convoy in in record time without loss and recommended a Bronze Star medal. After a few days, Kunming replied: "Give the medal to his executive officer." I never learned if Weiss actually received the decoration.

I was being treated like many other officers were treated who had gone out of style when Wedemeyer took over from Stilwell. I was additionally guilty of involvement in the effort to oust Chiang Kai-shek and Tai Li and to support the creation of a new middle-of-the-road government in China.

10 The City of Long Peace

Sian was the center of Chinese Nationalist authority in North China. The city was also called Changan, meaning Long Peace. But peace is something Sian has frequently been without during the past two thousand years.

The modern city of Sian lies on a rolling plateau near the Wei River, about fifteen miles from the Tsingling Mountains, which rise abruptly in a great green castellated barrier along the southern horizon. There is a fine old rectangular city wall built, according to local tradition, by Genghis Khan over six hundred years ago. The wall is cut in the middle of each face by gates, protected by magnificent towers which look toward the main points of the compass.

Inside the walls are wide streets which compare favorably in width with those of the better cities of the West. However, the inhabitants in 1945 had inherited little of Sian's imperial past. There were few old buildings and these were usually in deplorable condition. There was, for example, a famous old Confucian temple, known as the Peilin, or Forest of Tablets, which housed many old stone inscriptions; it should have been preserved both for its historic and intrinsic artistic merits, but it was rapidly mouldering away. There was once a fine imperial city in Sian where the Tang emperors held forth, and later the representatives of the Mongols, but nothing was left of this splendor but crumbling loess walls.

Sian had been sacked over and over again. Because it is situated at the edge of the Moslem areas, it has suffered through a succession of bitter religious wars. The people of the city, who numbered about four hundred thousand during World War II, were humbly housed in buildings of mud and brick. Except for a few pretentious modern structures, the city was an unimposing collection of homes and small shops built on the remains of a once great civilization.

The Wei River valley is one of the oldest centers of Chinese culture. The capital of the Chou dynasty, which established itself about the time of the traditional founding of Rome, was a few miles from Sian. Later the Han emperors, who ruled from two hundred years before the birth of Christ to about two hundred years after His death, built their capital on approximately the site of the present city. Still later, the northern Tangs had their capital here. The Mongols used Sian as one of their capitals after they conquered China.

The principal relics of this past greatness are, first, the walls and gate towers of the city and, secondly, the myriad tombs that dot the prairie for many miles around the city. Most of these are great earthen pyramids. There must be thousands of them and in some places they stretch as far as the eye can see. Many of them have never been opened.

I had the privilege of examining the exteriors of some of the larger tombs with Elissieff, a distinguished French archaeologist from the French National Museum. He maintained that hidden in these great mounds of earth is the world's greatest unexplored archaeological treasure. They were apparently built in this way: a great brick tomb was prepared and in it the body of the emperor was placed, together with whatever custom declared he should take with him to the afterworld. This often included hundreds of slaves, his wives and horses, and his personal treasure. Then the tomb was sealed and an immense mound of earth was piled over it in the form of a flat-topped pyramid.

We examined the tomb of the Han emperor who called himself P'ing Ling, or Hill of Peace. It was built on a platform about a thousand feet in diameter, was about seven hundred feet square at the base, and close to a hundred feet high. The central burial hall had caved in so that there was a crater on top.

A few of these pyramids have been robbed, and from them have come great bronzes and treasures in jade which have found their way to the museums of the world. However, these tombs have always been protected both by law and by popular superstition, and it is believed that most were untouched by robbers when the Communists established their government. Under the Nationalist regime, the tombs were protected by the Academia Sinica which forbade any archaeological excavation. Mao's government is reported to favor archaeology, and I hear several of these tombs have been systematically opened and the contents preserved for posterity.

Local customs vary greatly in different parts of China. I had always lived in South China except for a few months in the West, and I found Sian refreshingly new. There were many interesting characteristics of these northern people which I found attractive. They were perhaps poorer on the average, yet generally managed to maintain a high degree of personal cleanliness. I visited a little, one-room, loess-walled farmhouse and found it swept and garnished as neatly as any New England home could be. One of my friends was an old gentleman who sold rubbings—pictures made by printing from ancient sculptures—and his shop and home were immaculate.

Personal cleanliness is hard to maintain in a land where there is no public water supply and baths are bought at so much per bucket. The people of North China have an institution which I had read about in the *Arabian Nights* but never before encountered. Sian had a number of public bathhouses where the people who could afford to pay the price could bathe. These houses were of many kinds. Some apparently were brothels, but the better houses kept men and women segregated and were patronized by the best people in town.

I was persuaded to go to a bathhouse and had a thoroughly enjoyable experience, although a bit too strenuous in some respects. This house had been built before the war; it was equipped with porcelain tubs and had a number of tiled bathrooms. The upstairs was reserved for men and the downstairs for women. It was all quite proper.

We were hospitably welcomed and asked what kind of bath we wanted—first, second, or third class. We voted for the best and were escorted to a "private" room at the back of the building. On the way we passed the third-class bath, which was a large, tiled pool full of hot blue water, and the second-class room, which was a hall surrounded by booths where one could bathe and afterward relax in semiprivacy. Our room could have been a pleasant place but was not as clean as it should have been. There were two curtained alcoves on one side, each containing a tub. We were hustled into these by our male attendants who insisted that they should assist us.

"My, what a fine physique mine has," remarked my helper to the man who was supervising Bill Fenn's ablutions. The Chinese admire anyone who manages to put some flesh on his bones, and this was a tribute to the fact that I do not look like a victim of famine. "What a lovely white skin," was the next remark, and from that time on we were prodded and admired like prize cattle. The final act was a pedicure. I objected, but my man insisted.

He looked at my feet doubtfully. They had lived a couple of years in GI boots and had seen much trouble. "It's been a long time since you had a pedicure, hasn't it?" he asked. I agreed that it had indeed. I didn't tell him it was the first and probably would be the last time my feet were thus blessed.

We spent much of our spare time exploring the curio stores. Sian was remote enough to have avoided much tourist trade, and the area was sufficiently rich and ancient to have accumulated a large heritage of fine bronzes, porcelains, paintings, embroideries, rugs, and so on. Many of the old families had become impoverished and were selling their belongings in order to survive.

Not being experts, we all bought a certain amount of trash, yet those of us who dealt with the old established stores did pretty well. The Chinese businessman is as honest as the next man, and many during the war conscientiously endeavored to be fair to the Americans. Of course, there were others who were crooked, but the proportion of honest merchants seemed large.

There was one institution for which Sian soon became famous among Americans in China. That was the Temple of Ancient Origins, otherwise known as the Temple of Love. It was the only thing of precisely its type I ever saw in China. It consisted of a group of licensed houses centered about an old Buddhist temple. At first this was tolerated by the air force commander in Sian, who as the senior officer was in command of all Americans in the area. It is very cold in Sian in the winter, and many Americans went there because it was the only place in town where there were stoves. The place had long been a legitimate haven for travelers, and that may be the reason it eventually went into the business of prostitution.

Later it was declared out of bounds and was periodically raided by MP's. During this time we had many visiting firemen of various ranks from Washington. It was incomprehensible to me that so many of these, some of them officers of high rank, should insist on being taken to the Temple of Love and risk not only infection but military arrest.

The incidence of venereal disease, even in the best houses, was high. Two American captains one day were exploring another portion of Sian's extensive licensed area when they were approached by a delegation of girls who spoke through an interpreter: "Please tell our American allies that they should have nothing to do with us. We are all diseased. We do not wish to be the cause of harm to our American friends."

Sian was the key fortress of Northwest China. Whoever controlled Sian controlled more than a famous old city in a prosperous river valley. He controlled an important crossroads in central Asia. From Pearl Harbor to the fall of Japan, the situation in Northwest China was fairly stable. The troops of Marshall Hu Tsu-nan, representing the Generalissimo, held Sian and guarded the southern bend of the Yellow River. We believed he had some three hundred thousand men in his command —some of the best-equipped and best-trained men in the Nationalist armies.

In addition to these regulars, Hu exercised a nebulous control over many bands of Kuomingtang guerrillas operating back of the enemy lines. Some of these bands really fought the Japanese, but for the most part they seemed to function as advance guards against the penetration of the Communists into Nationalist territories. Hu had a good reputation as a general and was probably one of the better Chinese field commanders. He was assisted by General Fang, a Cantonese who was his chief of staff. Also on his staff and occupying a position of disproportionate influence was a Colonel Liu, who represented Tai Li.

There was for several years a three-cornered war in this part of China. Mao Tse-tung was in his fortress in Yenan and his guerrillas controlled large areas, both in Japanese and Kuomingtang territories. Everything east of Shensi province was supposed to be Japanese territory, but in fact they were restricted to the cities and to fortified camps at strategic points. Large areas were loyal to Chiang. Thus there were three political and military forces there who fought each other indiscriminately.

The Americans were caught in the middle. At first both Communist and Nationalist guerrilla bands cooperated with OSS. It was a common evening ceremony for most of our Sian detachment to jeep over to the Fourteenth Air Force base and take pictures of a sheepish young American standing in the doorless opening to our old beat-up C-46, together with one or more Chinese. They would be flown under cover of the night across the enemy lines only forty or fifty miles away until three bonfires were seen below. Our saboteurs would then be dropped in the triangle between the fires and would join guerrillas, Communists or Nationalists.

These groups carried radios, light weapons, and explosives. Some of them performed spectacular feats. One group lead by St. Cyr (who later described his exploit in the *Saturday Evening Post*) blew up the Yellow River bridge of the Peking-Hankow Railroad, inflicting a major defeat both on the Japanese and on the Tai Li forces who had consistently blocked efforts to destroy the interior lines of transportation of the enemy.

We learned at some cost that the Communists had turned against us. In the spring of 1945, we dropped several Americans, under a Major Coolidge, in a Communist-controlled area. They were arrested, disarmed, and imprisoned in loess caves for several weeks before their captors released them. They were threatened with death as enemies of the Chinese people. We attempted no further cooperation with Mao's forces.

Since I belonged to the discredited Stilwell-Donovan-Coughlin wing of OSS, I was not regarded as a desirable employee. Major Gustave Krause had known me in India and had the courage to invite me to join his command in Sian. I helped twice to bring large convoys up from Kunming to Sian. My chief duties were as a liaison with local Chinese. I was the only American on the base staff who spoke Chinese.

OSS had rented an empty compound outside the city of Sian from an American missionary society. A few small homes existed when we arrived. We contracted with Chinese builders to construct semipermanent barracks, warehouses, offices, and a central mess. I was caught in the middle between the Chinese and an arrogant racist executive officer. There were other officers and men who were contemptuous of all Chinese. I was almost constantly involved in smoothing things over after an American had been rude or sadistic to Chinese work-men, or to our neighbors, or to merchants inside the city walls.

There were other Americans who were as ashamed as I was of the anti-Chinese behavior of a minority of the men in our base. Several of them actively studied and collected Chinese bronzes, porcelain, paintings, ivory, lacquer, and rugs. Some of them bought excellent collections from the large stocks of antiques then available in the city. These men usually liked Chinese food and respected the Chinese people.

Each American officer had a Chinese interpreter whether he needed him or not. Mine was a Major Chen who went with me wherever I went. (It should be noted that there are only about one hundred Chinese surnames; Chen is one of the most frequently encountered of these names.) He was a Tai Li agent but as I got to know him better, I was convinced he was also a Communist, a double agent.

He had been educated in journalism and told me he had joined the Communist party while a university student. After graduation he was sent by the party to work on a newspaper. As assistant editor, he was able to slant the news and write editorials against the Kuomingtang. The paper was raided, he was arrested, and spent more than a year in a Tai Li correctional institution. Finally, he was able to convince his captors that he was completely brainwashed and would be a loyal worker for the Kuomingtang. So he became my interpreter. I don't think he wanted me to believe in his conversion. However, I was always cautious with him in case he tried to trap me for Tai Li.

He certainly was out to trap me. He was engaged to a pretty young nurse who shared an apartment with another equally pretty colleague. Several times I took Chen and the two girls out to dinner. Once we drove to a famous hot springs resort where Chiang Kai-shek had been kept a prisoner by Marshall Chang Hsueh-liang in 1936 until he promised to adopt a hard line with the Japanese; this was the immediate prelude to the Japanese invasion of China.

The unattached girl was a pianist, and sometimes the four of us would have dinner in their apartment after which she would accompany me on a rickety old piano as I sang folk songs and German lieder. A few days before Chen and his girl were married, I said to her while we were sitting alone by the piano: "It's going to be lonely for you after your friend is married."

She replied, "All right, then I'll sleep with you."

I never saw her again. I was convinced by many clues that Chen and the girls were Communists. It occurred to me that pianos were scarce in Shensi in 1945, and attractive girls who could play German lieder on the piano, and who were willing to sleep with an American officer must have been even more scarce.

Many years after World War II, I was visited in my office in Washington by two reporters from *Time* magazine who had been referred to me because I was supposed to have been well acquainted with John Birch, the patron saint of the society which bears his name. I was puzzled because he was blurred in my memories. When I first met John I think it was in my early days in Kunming—we seemed to share a love of China. We probably had several meals together. Thereafter I thought of him as a special friend, one of the few pepole I knew with whom I could communicate.

I remember John, who had just returned to Kunming from his dangerous post in the Anhwei pocket behind the Japanese lines, invited me to have dinner with him in a restaurant operated by refugees from Foochow. This city where I was born is famous for its distinctive cuisine. (The other four great Chinese cuisines are the Peking, Shanghai, West China, and Cantonese schools of cookery.) John ordered prawns caught in the Kunming Lake. We had several typical Foochow dishes with black mushrooms, golden needles, and familiar spices.

When I saw a radiogram reporting that he was coming to Sian for a special mission in North China, I was delighted. I met him at the airstrip and drove him to the OSS base where I tried to make him comfortable. I arranged to sit by him at meals and tried to talk to him. He made me very uncomfortable. He answered in monosyllables and his eyes were opaque. There was no communication at all between us. He seemed to be a changed man.

After a few days we took him out one evening to the airstrip and saw him aboard our plane which soon disappeared in the darkness to the east. None of us ever saw John again. A few weeks later, I was in our headquarters in Kunming waiting for transportation back home. I was with a group of my peers when one of them asked if we had heard that John Birch had been killed by the Communists.

A young lieutenant said, "It served him damn well right."

I replied, "That's a hell of a thing to say about a man who has done all he has done in this war, who was looking forward to going home to his family, and is killed after the war is over."

The lieutenant looked me in the eye and asked me if I had ever served with Birch. He had, and he said Birch was a sadist who loved to inflict pain, to beat the Chinese. If Birch had been shot by the Communists, the lieutenant thought he probably deserved it.

According to the answers I got from people who were in a position to know what really happened, John was somewhere in Shansi at V-J Day. Our people radioed him to go as fast as he could to a Japanese prisoner of war camp near Peking. There he was to demand the surrender of the camp. The commander was infamous for his treatment of allied prisoners. We were afraid he would shoot his prisoners to keep them from testifying at a war-crimes trial.

John Birch and a Chinese Nationalist major started toward Peking through a countryside controlled here by Nationalists, there by Communists, and over there by Japanese. They came to a roadblock where a Chinese Communist officer demanded to know who they were and where they were going. Birch lost his temper and began to slap the face of the Communist officer, who then ordered a soldier to shoot him. John fell mortally wounded. Then the Communists shot the Nationalist officer, who fell into the ditch and played dead. The Communist detachment withdrew. The Nationalist officer had a severe head wound and lost an eye, but managed to walk several miles to a Nationalist base, and was evacuated to a hospital where he reported the death of John Birch.

In retrospect, I doubt if I ever knew this man I had called my friend.

Paul Fanning was one of my more colorful friends in OSS. He was a veteran of the loyalist forces in the Spanish civil war. He was an actor and a playwright, and married to an actress. He was of medium height and swarthy enough to disguise himself as a Chinese. He spoke little or no Chinese; he was fond of good living, full of good stories, and apparently did not know how to be afraid.

He parachuted with a Chinese accomplice one night somewhere in Central Shansi province. He failed to find the guerrillas he expected to meet. He was disguised as a Chinese scholar, wore a long gown and Fu Manchu whiskers. His Chinese associate got a Peking cart which looked like a two-wheeled prairie schooner and was pulled by a team of mules.

For several weeks Paul and his friend managed to keep out of the hands of the Japanese. They would travel all night in the cart, then hide during the day, except when they were near fortified Japanese camps. Paul made an exhaustive photographic study of these camps, strolling around them holding his own hands hidden by loose sleeves, a posture affected by Confucian scholars. Paul had a Leica in those hands, and at convenient intervals he moved his sleeves and snapped pictures of the camps.

When these films were processed, it was discovered that these camps all were built in the same way; most of the garrison was clustered in a strong point at the eastern end of the camp, which was the place nearest to the homeland. The western part was lightly fortified and defended. This information was given to a reliable and

energetic Chinese Nationalist guerrilla leader, who succeeded in inflicting several defeats on the Japanese before they discovered and corrected the weakness in their
camps.

In the meantime, the Japanese suspected the presence of an American spy and Paul was continuously on
the move. He could not stop in the villages for food, and
reported by radio that all he had eaten for several weeks
was cucumbers stolen from the farms he passed at night.
Finally he reported that he was sick with something like
dysentery, had lost a lot of weight, and had to get out to
stay alive.

We had a council of war in Sian; it was impossible
to pick him up by plane, and we had no helicopters in
those days. His only chance was to slip past a series of
Japanese camps while traveling northwest to a point
below the place where the Yellow River bends south near
the edge of the Ordos Desert. At this point there is a
narrow gorge, and at that time there was supposed to be
a cable bridge made of vines across the river. These cable
bridges often were the only way to cross rivers in West
China.

We radioed Paul to cross that bridge and climb out
of the gorge to a small village held by Nationalists. I
volunteered to meet Paul there.

The only map we had was a Russian military map
which proved about 50 percent accurate. It looked to be
about four hundred miles from Sian to this place near
the northeast bend of the Yellow River. I was given a
quarter-ton weapons carrier, about two hundred gallons
of reserve gasoline, oil and a few spare parts, my choice
of weapons, and a surly and incompetent American radio

operator. Major Chen came along and was worth his weight in gold.

We had orders from Tai Li not to go more than twenty-five miles from Sian without special passports. There was no time to apply for them, and they would not have helped much anyway because we would pass close to Yenan and through Communist territory where the possession of Tai Li passes could have been dangerous.

The first large town we encountered was the traditional burial place of the Yellow Emperor who lived about 2700 B.C. His tomb is the biggest pyramid I have ever seen, now a large hill of loess. On one side the city wall looped across the hill, on the other about halfway up was a small temple near what appeared to be the mouth of a tunnel. I wanted to explore it, but while drinking tea in a restaurant we were accosted by a half-dozen very unfriendly Nationalist soldiers. They hurried off, presumably to get reinforcements, so we hurried on our way.

We passed through a rich valley where melons in profusion were ripening beside a clear river. In the valley was a sizable walled city. The road went straight through the city gate without any available detour. The gate was closed; when I honked a soldier opened it. I blithely drove through into a courtyard and faced a second wall and another closed gate. The one behind me slammed shut. I looked up and saw a Chinese soldier with a hand grenade which he was centering over my head. His eyes were preoccupied with the job of disposing of us. I broke into a tirade of profane gutter Chinese, denouncing him and his turtle-egg ancestry. He broke into a surprised grin and put the grenade away. In a few seconds he had descended the inside wall, opened the inner gate, and laughingly waved us on our way.

Our next barrier was a river. It was running high and the banks were muddy. A small scow was drawn up to the bank and an old man sat on it smoking a pipe. He said the ferry was not operating and he had no idea when it would start. I figured we were close to Communist territory. My Chinese major gave the old man a barely perceptible hand signal and the two men strolled out of earshot together. In a few minutes they strolled back and the ferry was in operation. It was barely big enough to accommodate the truck, and the swift current threatened to capsize us as the old man hauled us across on a cable.

During the summer of 1945, the Nationalists appeared to hold a number of large market towns in central and northern Shensi, while the high country seemed to be mostly Communist. The farther north we went, the fewer the Nationalists. Communist towns were clean, orderly, and rather empty. Nationalist towns were, in contrast, generally crowded, dirty, with lots of food in the shops. I stopped in a town northeast of Yenan to buy some eggs. I found none in several shops. Finally, an elderly shopkeeper said quietly, "Don't you understand that Communist hens don't lay eggs?"

We camped late the first evening in a meadow on a mountain. I tried to generate enough electricity on our hand-operated generator to enable my corporal to reach Sian on our spy-type radio. It apparently wasn't strong enough. We were never able to establish contact. I blamed it on my lazy, incompetent corporal. I felt almost as isolated as if I had been surrounded by a hostile army. We were in fact caught in the middle of a dormant civil war just beginning to come alive. Tension, unfriendliness, and a sense of danger followed us.

Near Yenan, the caravan trail, marked on our map as a road, climbed to a high plateau about seven thousand feet above the distant ocean. Here there were groves of pines, clear brooks, and very few people. The trail degenerated rapidly. Once we were stuck in the sand of a small river and were lucky to be able to winch our way ashore using the cable and winch on our weapons carrier.

Later we came to a large stream in arid country where the trail was cut out of a cliff above the river. Once I started over it there was no possibility of turning back. One section was so narrow that I drove the truck very slowly with the outside tire of the double-tired, rear, right wheel spinning slowly in space, while the left side of the truck scraped the cliff. I expected momentarily to plunge off into the rocky riverbed.

A few hours later, we bounced over a rocky pass and looked down into the deep gorge of the Yellow River. Below about the seven-thousand-feet level on both sides of the river, the country looked like true desert almost as forbidding as a moonscape. Directly below us was a small village of loess caves. In front of each cave was a garden plot protected by a low wall. A Chinese was waiting to guide me to a cave where I found Paul Fanning, thin and tired but in fine spirits. We toasted each other from a bottle I had brought for this purpose. Traveling as an unwanted third party in a country involved in an undeclared civil war is not pleasant.

The first night on our way home, we camped at a small grassy clearing in a pine forest on the high plateau.

A cold, clear brook ran nearby. Paul said he was starving for fresh meat, so I shot a big North China hare, almost as big as a jackrabbit. Paul said he would cook a dish he learned to like while he was fighting Franco in Spain. The rest of us preferred our field rations, and Paul ate the whole rabbit boiled with C-rations. A solitary man wandered down from a farmhouse but avoided conversation. According to our map, we were about thirty miles east of Yenan, and I assumed he would inform the Communists of our presence.

We slept on cots in the middle of the clearing in bright moonlight. I woke suddenly with a sense of danger. I thought I heard a number of men stealthily approaching through the woods. When they reached the edge of the clearing, they paused. I fired at the shadows with my .45. Something stumbled or fell into a sandy gulley, and there was a quiet retreat. The three men sleeping by me did not stir. I stayed awake the rest of the night. At daybreak, I was relieved to see no bloodstains at the place where somebody had apparently fallen into the gulley.

It was downhill all the way back to Sian through a countryside where nobody seemed to like us. I doubt if we could have gotten through without the presence of Major Chen.

11 Dubious Victory

Summer in Northwest China came abruptly in 1945. Soft winds and thunderstorms came with the southeast monsoons, and suddenly the trees were in full leaf, streams were high, fields were green, and snow departed from the mountains. Almost as rapidly came the signs of peace. The Japanese will to fight seemed to evaporate. Simultaneously, the latent hostility between the Communists and Nationalists began to erupt in isolated violence.

There was no danger now that our unarmed transport planes, our principal link through Kunming to Washington, would be shot down. We were visited by numerous, smartly uniformed young dandies from OSS in Washington. Most of them wanted to sample the soiled girls in the Temple of Ancient Origins, see something of the city of Sian, and stay long enough to qualify for a theater ribbon, with a bronze combat star.

We also had some of the same breed assigned to our detachment. They seemed to regret that the war was dying and lusted after opportunities to blood themselves. They wanted to participate in killing someone, and apparently they didn't care who it might be. Such opportunities were few but they made the most of them. Two involved separate groups of spies, three men and six girls. By this time we had an effective intelligence net across the Yellow River in Japanese territory. We were warned to expect these nine Japanese-trained Chinese spies on certain dates. We were still working under the SACO agreement and the Tai Li apparatus in Sian was reasonably cooperative in matters involved the detection of agents outside the Tai Li network. We would "interrogate" the spies and after we were finished with them, we would turn them over to the brutal mercies of Tai Li.

One young officer just out from Washington, the son of a well-known university president, who later became an ambassador, was eager to prove himself. Because of my language ability, he asked me to help him in the interrogations. I said I had had enough of brutality.

"The war's practically over," I said. "Why the hell don't you let them go? They don't know anything we need to know."

"They're spies, aren't they? And we're still at war. Anyway, if we turn them loose, Tai Li's boys will pick them up before they get far."

He was right, of course, and the senseless cycle of capture, "interrogation" by Americans, then by the Chinese, then execution, was repeated—but without my assistance.

Sometimes I wondered if anyone in Washington had read the top-secret report I had written at the suggestion of Mr. Chen nearly a year earlier. I had been so careful to avoid offending various sensibilities that, in retrospect, it seemed a fairly innocent statement. Nevertheless, it had recommended a basic change in American policies toward China, and suggested that we support those forces in China which, in turn, would actively support our objectives. I regretted sometimes that Colonel Coughlin had endorsed it and sent it on to Washington. I knew he had not been promoted and hoped his support of my paper had not hurt his career.

But every new development in China confirmed my conviction that the ousting of Stilwell and the victory of the Miles-Wedemeyer faction would end in disaster both

later, in a time and a place of their own choosing, the Communist world would force a showdown. In that time, America must have friends; without them we might not survive. We must be wiser and more cunning and more dedicated than the Communists, in the years ahead, if we were to survive. Soon he left, and I never saw him again.

Now we were preoccupied with two things, depending on our rank and temperament: getting home as quickly as possible, or gaining prestige by accepting a surrender.

There was a certain bird colonel in OSS who flitted about the world on mysterious missions. He made no secret of his political influence in Congress. Earlier in 1945, this colonel had visited OSS in Chungking. What he did I do not remember, but it caused an exchange of sharp messages in Washington. The colonel was put on a plane with one-way orders to Washington. In a short time, he was back in China; apparently somebody in Washington liked him—or wanted him on the other side of the world.

After the bombs at Hiroshima and Nagasaki, there was a pause which was neither peace nor war. In Korea, China, Formosa, and Southeast Asia, there were large, intact Japanese armies which had not surrendered.

The bird colonel arrived in Sian unexpectedly and informed my commanding officer, Krause, that our battered C-43 would be required for a one-way trip to Seoul, Korea. The colonel, accompanied by a small staff of his own choosing, would accept the surrender of the Japanese commanding general in Korea. Gus expostulated to no avail. A major normally does not talk back to a bird

colonel. Nobody in Washington or elsewhere had authorized the colonel to speak for his government in Korea or
anywhere else. So he took our plane and disappeared in
the direction of Korea. About twenty-four hours later, we
got word from the plane that the colonel and his crew
were on their way home to Sian.

They were glad to get back. The colonel reported his
exploit to Washington, presumably expecting some reward. It seems the Japanese in Korea weren't ready to
surrender. At first the Japanese commander was stiff,
and the troops at the airfield were trigger-happy. The
Japanese general told our colonel he had no authority to
surrender and that he feared for the safety of the American visitors. He urged immediate departure. The colonel
was agreeable, but pointed out that he lacked gas for the
thousand-mile return flight to Sian. So the general invited all the Americans to a banquet where there was
plenty of liquor and many toasts. The colonel proposed a
toast to Emperor Hiroshito with whom we were technically still at war. After the dinner, the Americans found
their plane had been serviced and flew home. All this,
the colonel reported to Washington. The next day a
stinging message arrived from Washington. The colonel
was to consider himself under arrest and would return
immediately to Washington.

Later I was edified by evidence that you just can't
keep a good man down. He turned up in Manila where
he was in charge of the disposal of U.S. surplus property
worth hundreds of millions. The odor from this operation
was wafted all the way to New York and aroused the
interest of a national news weekly. It became wise for
the colonel to leave the Philippines without stopping over

in Washington. The last I heard of him, years later, he was living in Thailand with a bevy of beautiful Thai girls.

My orders came to start for Kunming and home. I left Gus Krause and Sian with real regret. In Kunming relations between Americans and Chinese were deplorable. There were numerous reports of Americans, individually and in groups, being robbed and killed by Chinese. Americans were under standing orders not to carry arms because they were guests of their Chinese allies. I always carried a .32 in a shoulder holster regardless of orders.

One night Phil Crowe, a good friend from the New Delhi days, asked me to go for a walk in the old city of Kunming. We were cornered by five Chinese soldiers chanting *"sha, sha,"* meaning "kill, kill." I pulled my pistol, held its muzzle down by my leg, yelled Chinese obscenities at the men, and Phil and I walked through them without harm. The difference between us and the Americans who were found dead in the Kunming streets was my illegal pistol.

After twenty-five years, I still remember some of the men I knew in OSS as among the best I have ever met. Many of them still awe me: Bill Morgan, a middle-aged Ph.D. in psychology who somehow wrangled himself successively into the army, into the paratroopers, through officers training school, into OSS, and into a dangerous drop in France, where he joined the French underground, although he spoke very little French, and became a scourge of the Gestapo. He married a beautiful English girl at Oxford, but volunteered for new hazardous duty in China after the collapse of Germany.

There were many others, of all ages, sizes, and characters. One swashbuckler I cannot forget was Leonard

Clark, explorer, mystic, warrior. We had a date after the
war to climb Amne Machin, a mountain in northern
Tibet I had photographed years earlier. Len and I both
believed it to be higher than Everest. Len did go to Amne
Machin after the war on foot and took photographs of
the mountain which were published in *Life*. A bit later
he went to South America on some mysterious mission
and drowned in a rapids.

There was much glory to be gotten by accepting sur-
renders. Miles's navy outfit and various army organizations competed for chances to accept surrender swords
from defeated Japanese samurai. There was one great
plum remaining—General Hondo and his three hundred
thousand men in Formosa. As I remember, we hatched
this plan at a poker game: Ten of us under Leonard
Clark, with the experienced Bill Morgan as ballast, would
parachute onto the airfield at Taipei and invite Hondo to
surrender. Incredibly, the plan was approved.

Of course no one had any assurance that Hondo
wanted to surrender, and there was no way to communicate with him. We would jump over the airfield while
the radio on the plane explained who we were and why
we were coming. After that, there would be a few minutes of breathless prayer and the moment of truth.

I wanted desperately to be part of this mission, to
finish my military career in a brief moment of nonfrus-
tration, but it was not to be. When the boys took off for
Taipei one night, I was in an army hospital with a bad
back. I had asked that it be examined, and taped if necessary, before the jump. The doctors took me out of the
game. Years later, Bill Morgan tracked me down to give
me one of the samurai swords surrendered by Hondo's

officers. He also flattered me by inviting me to be god-father of one of his sons.

While in the hospital, I took stock of the past two years: obviously I had not been created to be a soldier. But I was deeply grateful for the experiences I had had and for the chance to be part of the weird and wonderful organization known as the Office of Strategic Services. As for China, and for Sino-American relations, I could see only darkness ahead. America had won a war with Japan, and lost one in China.

Epilogue

OSS in Washington amazed me. We lived at the Congressional Country Club while we were being mustered out. The luxury was easy to enjoy.

One day I received an invitation to meet a colonel for lunch in the Pentagon. He turned out to be an older professional soldier somehow connected with the Chief of Staff. He introduced me to four other colonels. They told me they were jointly authorized to offer me a top position in G2 (Military Intelligence), with responsibility, rank, and authority to revamp our entire military intelligence structure in the Far East. They promised me a promotion to higher rank in the regular army, additional quick promotions, and the full support of the army.

I was stunned. I asked them why they were making me such an offer. They said they had all read a report I had written in China, and it represented the kind of thinking which was going to be needed in the postwar period.

I said I was greatly honored and wanted a little time to think about their proposal. However, I was concerned about the possibility that I might accept this offer, then find myself working for some general who did not share my ideas. This might happen, they said; it was the risk all officers must face. But it was unlikely that the army would revert to earlier policies in Asia. They believed I would have a good opportunity to help to reshape military intelligence policy. The first colonel gave me his address and urged me to write him when I had made up my mind.

I went home to my family for a few weeks and wrote the colonel that I was interested in his proposal. Orders arrived for me to go to Fort Dix for the tests and

processing required for the integration of a reserve officer in the regular army. The first day at Fort Dix went
according to the script. On the second day, a young briga-
dier general informed me that I was at liberty to go home.
I would be advised of the army's decision. I heard no
more.

Years later, when I was assistant commissioner of
education in the U.S. Office of Education, I went to Sche-
nectady, New York, as guest of the superintendent of
schools. During a conversation with several people on
his staff, we got around to discussing China, and I described the paper I had written for Colonel Coughlin to
send to OSS recommending support for a new moderate
government to replace Chiang Kai-shek and hopefully to
head off the Communist conquest of China.

"I know all about that paper," said one of the men.
"I was Wild Bill Donovan's secretary."

He told us this story: Donovan took the paper to
Roosevelt, who seemed to agree with my thesis. The president called a cabinet meeting to discuss the China situation. There seemed to be a consensus that Chiang could
not hold China together and the United States should
support the formation of a new, moderate, pro-American
government. Then Admiral Leahy made a strong statement in favor of Chiang: We must not stab this old
friend in the back. The president polled the cabinet, and
Leahy and Chiang won by a narrow margin.

Stilwell died not long after his removal from the Far
East. Some reports said he died of cancer; others suspected a broken heart.

Tai Li returned to Nanking with the Generalissimo.
For a time he rode very high. An article in an American

monthly described him as one of the most powerful men in China, and possibly in the postwar world. One day Tai Li took off from Nanking in his airplane. It exploded in midair. A man who could have known the facts told me an OSS limpet (magnetic) bomb might have been attached to an engine on his plane.

In 1944 and 1945, America insisted on continuing to support Chiang Kai-shek, who already was being repudiated by his people. A few years later, hundreds of thousands of American-trained-and-equipped Nationalist troops turned against Chiang and joined the victorious Communist armies. Today, in 1971, we support the myth that Formosa is the Republic of China.

For a century Americans have supported landlords and mandarins in East Asia. We have seen what we wanted to see, believed what we wanted to believe about the peoples and governments of East Asia. If the Chinese people and the American people learn to trust each other and work together, there is a fair chance for world peace during the balance of this century. Without peace, the future of all is in danger. The greatest single challenge to the people of America today is to overcome the mistakes of past generations, and our distrust of the Oriental, and to cultivate a new understanding with the peoples of China.

Sino-American relations since 1900 have been a love-hate relationship, perhaps unique in international affairs. On the American side, it has been emotional and irrational. This accounts for the savage, personal attacks on Americans who have dared to oppose unquestioning American support for the Chinese Nationalist government.

The Communist victory and the flight of Chiang and his party and what was left of his armies to Formosa was followed by a witch hunt to find Americans to blame for Chiang's defeat. General George C. Marshall, together with a few China specialists, including Davies, Service, Atcheson, and Lattimore, became scapegoats.

Until very recently we have been committed as a nation to a ridiculous charade which maintains that the legitimate government of seven hundred million Chinese resides in Formosa. We have "loved" the Chinese in Formosa and "hated" the Peking government of the Chinese Communist Party. We ceremonially "unleashed" the Formosan armies and expected them to reconquer the continent which originally had spewed them forth. We have acted like demented elderly aunts in our dealings with Peking, a world power destined to become more powerful and more dangerous.

I suggest the irrational character of Sino-American relationships is the result of deep similarities as well as differences in the characters of the two peoples; both sides are afflicted by profound racisms.

Sino-American friendship and cooperation has been hampered by mutual racial prejudice. Most Americans and Chinese insist in looking down on each other. Mao has exploited this mutual fault to build his own strength, and in so doing has strengthened in Washington attitudes quite as irrational as his own.

An American who grew up in China was caught between two racisms. Most Americans living in pre-Communist China were living on two levels. They had their own circle of Chinese friends with whom they dealt as equals; but other Chinese were somehow not fully human.

This assumption is illustrated by the situation in the International Settlement in Shanghai. Americans held the balance of power in the foreign community. For years an American held a position similar to that of mayor in an American city. Shanghai was full of evidence of good American intentions, such as two universities, many schools and churches, hospitals, and various social welfare projects. But Americans did not insist on the removal of the signs in the Bund Gardens which said in Chinese and English: "Chinese and Dogs not Allowed." I saw no evidence of any determined American effort to improve intolerable working conditions in the cotton mills, to end the chattel slavery of thousands of young girls sold each year to the licensed houses, or to improve the condition of thousands of rickshawmen, who were believed to have an average life expectancy of three years while working as human horses.

We justified ourselves by blaming the Chinese—but they had no jurisdiction in the International Settlement. In justice, it must be said that conditions were often as bad in the Chinese areas of Shanghai. Shanghai was correctly described as a cancer on the face of China.

Chinese racism is deeply rooted in Chinese history. For five thousand years China was the Middle Kingdom, a civilized oasis surrounded by barbarians. The Chinese have little body hair, but most of their neighbors are hairy; therefore hairy people are inferior. The Chinese are a lightly pigmented people; most of the neighboring barbarians are either lighter or darker; therefore white people and black people are barbarians.

Much has been made of the ability of the Chinese to assimilate their invaders. Even the Jewish communities in China have almost entirely disappeared. Chinese racism may be more sophisticated and less brutal than American and European racism. But the Chinese are capable of racial violence. There was a long and bloody record of murders of small groups of Americans and Europeans in China. One of my earliest memories involves a screaming mob of Chinese chasing a solitary black Indian Sikh with intent to kill.

More characteristic of Chinese racism were harmless instances which occurred when we were traveling as a family in rural areas. When we stopped to rest, we would be surrounded by curious and friendly people. We frequently heard these remarks:

"Why do these people smell so bad? They smell like foxes."

"They smell that way because they eat beef."

Beef was not often eaten by rural Chinese, and it was also true that Chinese are not much afflicted by body odor.

One of the strangest expressions of racism in China before Mao was in the Christian churches, both Catholic and Protestant. During the nineteenth century, and up to about 1930, there was a slow growth of the Christian community to about three million avowed Chinese Christians, two-thirds of them Catholic. But there were two levels of the Christian priesthood or ministry. Lebbe, a Belgian Vincentian father, made it his lifework to bring equality into the priesthood. When he arrived in China, Chinese priests were treated as socially inferior to European priests. He suffered years of exile before he finally convinced Rome that there could not be a caste system in the priesthood. Through his efforts, the first Chinese bishop was appointed in the early 1930s. Paul Yu-pin later became the first Chinese cardinal. The Protestant churches were also afflicted by racism, but they may have made more of an effort to develop Chinese Christian leadership. Nevertheless, the first Chinese Methodist bishop was not appointed until the 1930s.

American churches spent millions to convert the heathen Chinese. But when our missionary family returned to America on furlough, school became a purgatory for me, as it was for many other American children born in China. My first memory of an American public school was the chant which greeted me every morning: "Chinky, Chinky Chinaman." The cruelty of children reflects the prejudices of their parents.

But the American people have come a long way in a generation. Tens of thousands of Oriental war brides and the admission of Hawaii to statehood have resulted in deep changes in the status of Americans of Oriental background. Unfortunately, I see no corresponding improvement in public American attitudes toward the peoples of Asia.

The failure of Americans and Chinese to cooperate effectively during World War II was in part a result of mutual racial antipathy. In Chengtu, in Kunming, Chungking, and elsewhere, I became aware of a strong undercurrent of dislike and suspicion of Americans. I had never before seen so much Chinese racial prejudice. But we frequently earned the dislike of the Chinese people.

In World War II, and also in Korea and Vietnam, Americans overseas quickly wore out their welcome. The fault has often been our own. In China, as in North Africa, India, and elsewhere, the chief source of difficulty was sexual. There were too many Americans who considered all foreign women fair prey.

While I was a soldier in China, it was always a special trial to play host to visiting firemen from Washington. There were always some in each group who wanted women. They had no manners, no sensitivity, and made enemies for the rest of us.

At one time, circumstances required me to be frequently on the streets of Sian with two American officers. In our billets, they were intelligent and pleasant people. On the streets they were a constant source of humiliation, making obscene proposals in English to upper-class women, many of whom understood too well what was being said to them. English had been, for many years, a required subject in Chinese schools.

In Chengtu two graduates of Yenching University, the great American university at Peiping, set themselves up in the restaurant business. They wanted, first, to make money and, secondly, to serve the American troops. Their restaurant was one of the best I saw in China. The food was excellent and the prices were low. The place became popular and the two hosts were always ready to do anything they could to help their American guests.

One day they came to ask my advice. The previous night, after the restaurant had closed, there had been a great banging on the doors downstairs. A group of Americans were demanding admission.

"We have closed," said one of the proprietors in excellent English.

"We don't want to eat. We want women," was the answer.

"There are no women here," protested the proprietor.

The Americans would not go away for a long time, but kept banging on the doors and shouting obscenities until the entire block was awake and the neighbors were shouting imprecations.

What should they do in such circumstances, I was asked. And what could I answer? If the MP's were available, they should be called, but MP's seldom were around when they were needed.

GI drivers frequently developed a completely calloused attitude toward the lives and the properties of Chinese. One GI truck driver told me his previous officer had said to his men, "I don't care how many of the slopeys you hit, but when you run into them, be sure to kill them. I don't want them to live to complain to me." When this driver joined my convoy, he very quickly learned another set of rules.

The Chinese drink a lot and get drunk as often as other men, but they follow certain conventions. You can live in China for years and never see a drunken Chinese on the streets. They get drunk in private. But it was a common sight to see American officers and men in the streets with half-empty bottles in their hands. As they grew drunk, they became increasingly abusive, lecherous, and otherwise obnoxious. The spree often ended in a brawl.

The situation was exploited by Tai Li's forces and other hostile elements working secretly to destroy the basis of Sino-American military cooperation by magnifying American faults. Chinese women in country areas were told that Americans had certain horrifying biological peculiarities which made them different from other men. The result was that many country girls would run from Americans as if they had seen a tiger. I suspect, however, that this propaganda backfired in some instances.

Chinese racism showed itself in a haughty unwillingness of many upper-class Chinese to meet the Americans socially. It was difficult for Americans to meet decent women. While I was in Chengtu, there was a typical incident of this type. The U.S. Army Air Force had leased part of the spacious University Hospital, and the army wing was under a regular army colonel. He was frequently harrassed by the anti-American racial prejudices of the Chinese doctor in charge of the university part of the hospital.

The army hospital was short of nurses. The three American nurses present were under a severe strain. Most of the care of the patients had devolved on ignorant GI's who had not been trained for the job. However, Colonel McKissick considered that it would be unethical to lure away the Chinese nurses next door by offering higher salaries.

Some of these nurses were pretty and not averse to polite American company, so they were invited to attend the GI movies which were given several times a week. When the movies were over, they would return to their quarters. Under such an arrangement, the opportunities for fun and games were virtually nonexistent, but the Chinese hospital superintendent decreed that any Chinese nurse who accepted an invitation to see the army movies would immediately be dismissed. This was too much for the colonel. He stormed into the superintendent's office and said, "You fire them and I'll hire them." The threat was enough. The nurses went to the movies.

Most American soldiers did not understand that possibly nowhere else in the world was there the same free and easy comradeship between men and women that is found in America. Most American girls have been conditioned all their lives to take care of themselves. They can say NO, and are not mortally offended if they have to say it. Women in other countries, and especially in conservative China, were accustomed to an entirely different way of life.

There was an elderly gentleman of my acquaintance, a Christian, who said to me, "In the old days, not so long ago, we had a good custom. If a young man had reason to believe that his bride was not a virgin, he would send his wife home. Her father would then bury her alive under the floor of the kitchen, and everyone would forget that she had ever lived. I think we should do the same today." I believe he spoke for a large segment of Chinese society.

Prostitutes abounded almost everywhere in China during the war. A Chinese can tell one kind of woman from another and does not make enemies by insulting "good" women. Americans in China seemed to be unable to distinguish, or perhaps they just did not care because of their contempt for "slopeys."

There was an American who seduced the wife of a Chinese officer. She had three children. She was desperately in love with the American. When he got tired of her, he arranged to be transferred to another post and left her with a small sum of money. Her husband would have nothing more to do with her.

I knew a dashing American who won a beautiful college girl and lived with her until V-J Day. Then he told the girl he was planning to return to America to his wife. I heard her quietly inform him that she would kill him if he tried to leave her. I left before the end of this story.

There should have been a training center where all personnel bound for China would be processed. Here they would have been told the truth about conditions in China, would have learned how to behave themselves, and perhaps how to live off the land and like it. They should have been tutored in Mandarin so that each man would have had a few essential words and phrases. Such preliminary training was practical and would have done much to improve Sino-American relations. It should have been backed up with rigid discipline. General Stilwell and his staff in Chungking did try to enforce such discipline. Senior officers sometimes got out of line themselves and would not or could not control their men.

All in all, I believe American troops in China generally behaved themselves as well as any army has behaved. Even the best of armies has disciplinary problems. These problems were exploited for propaganda purposes by unscrupulous forces in China.

Anti-American cliques fleeced the American forces in China out of hundreds of millions of dollars. The official exchange rate between Chinese and American money varied from about twenty Chinese dollars for one American dollar in the beginning of American participation in the war to about eighty to one at the end. Meanwhile, the actual value ranged from eighty to one at the beginning to over three thousand to one near the end. Certain Chinese government officials made great fortunes out of this arrangement. If Americans wished to buy land and to erect a building, they would pay for the land, the labor, and the material at twenty or forty or eighty to one, whereas the Chinese middlemen, or whoever actually handled the money, would buy at the open market rate.

The bricks of a certain OSS building in Kunming were said to have cost a dollar each in American money. The actual value of the bricks was possibly five cents. Someone made a clear profit of about ninety-five cents on each brick.

Only near the end of the war did the Americans begin to rebel, to insist on exchanging their official funds themselves, and on handling their own building. This improvement occurred only in certain outlying cities where the Service of Supply of the United States Army did not function, where smaller agencies of the army could handle their own affairs.

The exchange problem operated to the advantage of individual troops because they were able to multiply their incomes many times by buying Chinese money on the presumably illegal "open" market. Even so, their money did not go far. Frequently the Chinese press would blast the American authorities for permitting their men to buy Chinese currency at black market rates, yet prices were so high that a good dinner in a restaurant in Chungking or Kunming would cost more dollars at the most favorable black market rate of exchange than most GI's could afford. Americans would have found it almost impossible to live in China if they had been forced to rely on legal exchange.

I believe the Chungking government was dominated by nationalists who did not like America and American ideas. They had decided to let America win the war without their help and to make as much money as possible in the process. Many in this group would have been pleased to see America defeated. They were loyal to China to the extent that they were determined that China would be on the winning side.

In spite of mutual prejudice, American influence in China was great for two or three generations. This influence was deep-rooted; it was built on the multitude of schools, hospitals, churches, and cultural institutions that the American people gave to China, and on the millions of lives saved by American famine relief programs. This was what Wendell Wilkie called a "Reservoir of Goodwill."

The conservative elements in Chiang's government did not like Americans and their ideas. The application of these ideas to the solution of China's economic and social problems might have saved China from Mao Tse-tung. The Chinese Communist leadership understood this very well, so the Americans were attacked by both the Right and the Left. Our only hope in China was to make an alliance with a new moderate government. This is what Mr. Chen tried to tell me and I tried to tell Washington.

Index of Names